TO THE HEBREWS

TO THE HEBREWS

A DOGMATIC AND DEVOTIONAL COMMENTARY

BY

BEDE FROST

A. R. MOWBRAY & Co. LIMITED
LONDON AND OXFORD
MOREHOUSE-GORHAM CO.
NEW YORK

First published in 1947

PRINTED IN GREAT BRITAIN BY
A. R. MOWBRAY & CO. LIMITED, LONDON AND OXFORD
7131

CONTENTS

CONTENTS

TO THE HEBREWS

INTRODUCTION

THIS Introduction is concerned with furnishing the
modern reader of *Hebrews* with such information as
may awaken interest in, and stimulate appreciation of,
its value both from the dogmatic and the practical point
of view. Such details and points of controversy as are of
interest only to scholars are omitted, as being of little
consequence to those who desire to understand the writer's
message to those whom he addresses, amongst whom the
Christian of to-day has his place. For whilst S. Paul's
words, 'Every Scripture inspired of God is also profitable
for teaching, for reproof, for correction, for instruction in
righteousness: that the man of God may be complete,
furnished completely unto every good work,'[1] primarily
refer to the writings of the Old Testament, they are no
less true of those of the New.

1. *The Author of the Epistle*

The fact that no extant manuscript bears any name has
led to endless conjecture, from the earliest days until the
present time, as to the identity of its author. The Fathers
of the Eastern Church almost unanimously attribute it
to S. Paul, whilst, up to the fourth century, those of the
West as unanimously deny, or question, his authorship.
This difference of opinion arose from the fact that the
style, the language, the way in which the writer quotes
from the Old Testament,[2] the whole presentation of

---

[1] 2 Tim. iii. 16, 17.
[2] Unlike S. Paul, he quotes always from the Septuagint or Greek
version, never from the original Hebrew.

the subject, have no parallel in the Apostle's writings. In modern times, almost every name mentioned in the New Testament, and some not found there, has had its supporters, but the fact remains that we know no more than did Origen (A.D. 183–253), when he wrote, 'If I gave my opinion I should say that the thoughts are those of the Apostle [i.e. S. Paul], but that the phraseology and the composition belong to some one who was reporting his teachings, as might a scholar writing down the words of his master. Any Church, then, that considers this Epistle as coming from Paul is to be congratulated; for it is not by chance that the ancient Fathers have handed it down to us as his. But who wrote the Epistle? God knows the truth.'[1]

We may note that this distinction between the author and the actual writer of the Epistle was sanctioned by the Biblical Commission at Rome in 1914, and also, that this question of authorship in no way affects the canonicity of the Epistle. The Church, whose right it is, has decided to include it amongst those books of the New Testament Scriptures which are to be held as inspired by God, and to be read as an authentic and trustworthy record of His supreme revelation to men. The disputes and questionings of Biblical critics as to who wrote this or any other book of Holy Scripture have nothing to do with the fact of their canonicity.

The Epistle itself gives us some scraps of information about its writer. If he was not an actual member of the community to which he writes, he was well known to it, had visited it, and was hoping to return there.[2] He was fully aware of the conditions under which his readers had been and were now living,[3] of the imperfect character of their faith,[4] and of the discouragement and slackness from which some of them were suffering.[5] The authorita-

[1] Eusebius, *Ecclesiastical History*, vi. 13, 14.   [2] Heb. xiii. 19, 23.
[3] ibid., vi. 9, 10; x. 32–34.   [4] ibid., v. 11–14.
[5] ibid., vi. 11, 12; x. 23–25; xii. 14–17.

tive tone which runs through the Epistle seems to spring, not only from a deep conviction of the truth which he enunciates, but also from the knowledge that his readers will recognize his right to address them in so apostolic a manner.

We may picture him, then, sitting down, perhaps with some scribbled shorthand notes, or with a vivid remembrance, of S. Paul's teaching, to write 'this word of exhortation . . . in few words' to his sorely beset brethren in that province of the Empire already overshadowed by the clouds of persecution and the growing menace of civil war and invasion.[1]

2. *To Whom was it Written?*

The only clues we have as to the destination of the Epistle, and to the circumstances which occasioned its writing, are to be found in the Epistle itself. It would appear that the word Hebrews used in the title does not apply to the race, or to Jewish converts to Christianity in general, but to a particular community of Jewish Christians living in Jerusalem, or in some town of Palestine, most probably between A.D. 64–66, that is, some thirty years after the first preaching of the Gospel by the Apostles. The date is significant. In A.D. 66 the hatred of the Jews against their Roman oppressors, already manifested in one ineffectual rising after another, broke out in strength. Jerusalem was occupied by the patriots, the Roman garrison massacred, an attempt by the Twelfth Legion to recover the city was defeated, and the Christians fled across the Jordan seeking safety. The following year the Roman general Vespasian invaded Galilee with a

---

[1] I am not unaware of the modern critical theories as to the destination of the Epistle, and of the particular occasion which evoked it. I can see no valid reason for preferring any one of them to that which both the Epistle itself and Christian tradition seem to indicate. They form an apt illustration of that marked tendency in recent criticism, not only of the Bible, of which it has been said, 'In the present age it has become a fashionable practice in criticism first to conjure a theory from the nebular spaces of the mind and then to adjust the evidence to support the theory.'

large army, and on August 1, A.D. 70, Jerusalem was captured after a siege of one hundred and forty-three days, the city and Temple laid in ruins, and the few survivors sold into slavery, or sentenced to die by the gladiators' swords in the arena, the 'sports stadium' of the time.

The Epistle does not lack indications that the writer had some knowledge of the unsettled, and rapidly deteriorating, situation in which his friends are living. The persecution from which they were suffering may have proceeded, not only from purely religious motives, but also from nationalistic ones. For we know that there were many Jews who refused to take part in the revolt of A.D. 66, and perished at the hands of their own countrymen.

The Temple is still standing, and the ancient worship being offered;[1] there is no suggestion that the Christian Jews have fled across the Jordan; and nothing said which implies the revolt of A.D. 66, much less of the fall of Jerusalem which, had it occurred, would have been so strong a confirmation of the writer's argument designed to show that the old Mosaic Law and Covenant had been brought to a decisive and final end.

The Epistle leaves us in little doubt as to the circumstances which determined its writing. Some members of a group of Jewish Christians, who had been converted during the early days of the apostolic preaching, were now contemplating, under the stress of renewed persecution, a return to Judaism. Added to the fact of persecution (which, as we have said, may have been induced by political as well as religious motives), there was the sense of isolation from the still existent glory of the Temple worship which they had abandoned for the hole-and-corner assemblies of their new Faith. This sense would be accentuated by the rapidly growing belief, fostered by the underground nationalist party, that the day was at hand when the Roman domination, with its increasing menace to the ancient religion, would be swept away.

[1] Heb. viii. 4, 5; x. 2, 11.

But these factors which struck from without were reinforced, and that more dangerously, by one within themselves. It would seem that their conversion had been more
of an emotional act than one dictated by reason, and
although it had been strong enough to endure persecution
in the past, it had not led to that growth in the knowledge
of the Faith which was to be expected, and which was
indispensable in this new crisis which beset them. Their
early fervour was wearing away; the Apostles were gone
from them; community of fellowship and worship no
longer bound them solidly together; doubts and fears
brought despondency and slackness and the consequent
weakening of their once high resolve; the very emotional-
ism which had largely motived their acceptance of the
Gospel now threatened to betray them into apostasy from
the Faith.

It is with all this in his mind that the writer sits down
to compose this Epistle in which he mingles teaching,
warning, exhortation, and encouragement, in the endeavour to make them realize the gravity of the sin with
which they are temporizing, the certainty of the truth
they are in danger of forsaking, and the need of such a
renewal of their faith as shall inspire them to meet whatever may befall them from without with steadfastness,
patience, and confidence.

3. *The Position of Hebrews in the New Testament*

We know that the books of the New Testament are not
arranged in chronological order, but in one of dignity,
the Gospels being given the first place, although some of
the Epistles had been written, and were in circulation,
before the Synoptic Gospels, and are thus not dependent
upon them, nor upon S. John's, which appeared much
later. Thus they are witnesses to the existence of a
tradition of Christian faith and practice which does not
derive from the Gospels, but from the oral preaching and
teaching of the Apostles whom our Lord had chosen, and

to whom He had committed the promulgation of the Truth which He was, and had revealed.

In the order in which the Epistles occupy *Hebrews* stands as a fitting, one might almost say, necessary appendix to those which precede it. For, as Aquinas has pointed out, while *Romans*, *Galatians*, and *Corinthians* treat mainly of the Christian life in the individual, *Ephesians*, *Philippians*, and *Colossians* of the same life in the mystical Body of Christ, the Church, and the Pastoral Epistles of those who minister that life, in *Hebrews* we have an Epistle which, after reasserting the divine Personality and true Humanity of Christ, is devoted to an exposition of His Priesthood and Sacrifice, by which He has become the Mediator of the New Covenant between God and man.

Thus this Epistle fills in, completes, and illustrates the knowledge we gain from other New Testament writings concerning the Personality of Christ and more especially His High-priestly Office, and in doing so is seen to be at one with those other writings, and so to afford us a clear and definite picture of the Faith as held by Christians of the first century of our era.

4. *The Epistle and the Modern Reader*

Hebrews presents certain difficulties to the twentieth-century reader which would not have been experienced by those of the first and succeeding centuries. These difficulties, at least to the Christian, are not so much concerned with the doctrines which the writer emphasizes, as with the arguments and illustrations with which he endeavours to justify and support them. And this is be-cause they are drawn from, and coloured by, the history, beliefs, and practice of a Judaism which, to greater or less extent, is foreign to us. We move, as it were, in a strange country, in an atmosphere of thought and ideas which is so unfamiliar as to create an impression of unreality. This is more acute than it was to our forefathers whose know-ledge of the whole Bible was so much greater than that possessed by many to-day. We should probably get a somewhat similar impression if we compared a volume of present-day sermons with one containing those of the Fathers, preachers in the Middle Ages, or, indeed, of English divines of the seventeenth or eighteenth centuries. For those of English preachers, like those of earlier ages, are filled with quotations from every part of the Bible, many of them in the Latin of the Vulgate version, and of ideas now almost completely forgotten. If we are to understand and appreciate them we must do as when we desire to understand and appreciate Greek or Latin literature, the plays of Shakespeare or Sheridan, that is, gain some knowledge of the thought and customs of the age in which they were written, and which they reflect. So must it be with Hebrews, although here our task is easier, since the chief source of our knowledge is ready at hand in the Bible itself. Hence the numerous references found in the ensuing commentary which the author begs readers to look up and read as they occur.

The modern reader, unlike those to whom the Epistle was addressed, and to Christians of earlier times, often finds difficulty in following and appreciating what is known as the mystical and spiritual, or typical sense of Holy Scripture. Since Hebrews, in common with the rest of the New Testament writings, assumes such mystical interpretation to be both valid and valuable, a few words of explanation of its meaning and use may be welcome to some readers.

The New Testament writers regard the Old Testament Scriptures as having both a literal, historical sense, and a spiritual sense, that is, a meaning which goes beyond the literal sense, and signifies spiritual realities. This does not imply that the Old Testament writers were themselves conscious of the spiritual significance of what they recorded; only that, guided and inspired of God, they did in fact write of persons, things, and events of their own time which were types or figures of persons, things, and

events of the Christian, supernatural order. Thus the
writer of Hebrews speaks of the Mosaic Law as 'having a
shadow of the good things to come, not the very image
of the things'[1] where 'shadow' means the unsubstantial
image or copy as contrasted with the true Image, Who is
our Lord, Who contains within Himself the full substance
and reality to which the Law pointed.[2] So also the tabernacle of old is a type of the 'true tabernacle which the
Lord pitched, not man';[3] the Aaronic priesthood 'serve
that which is a copy and shadow of heavenly things';[4]
by the entry of the high priest alone into the Holy of
holies on the Day of Atonement 'the Holy Ghost signifieth
that the way into the Holy Place [that is, heaven] hath not
yet been made manifest,' until Christ entered 'not into a
Holy Place made with hands, like in pattern to the true,
but into heaven itself.'[5]

Such mystical interpretation of the Old Testament
Scriptures has the authority of our Lord Himself. 'Ye
search the Scriptures because ye think that in them ye
have eternal life; and these are they which bear witness
of Me.'[6] 'Beginning from Moses and from all the prophets, He interpreted to them in all the Scriptures the
things concerning Himself.'[7] 'These are My words which
I spake unto you, while I was yet with you, how that all
things must needs be fulfilled which are written in the
Law of Moses, and the prophets, and the psalms, concerning Me.'[8] It is not surprising, then, to find the
Apostles interpreting the Old Testament in the same way,
seeing on every page the shadow of Christ, His office, and
kingdom.[9]

So does the author of Hebrews find Christ spoken of

[1] Heb. x. 1.
[2] Cf. ibid., i. 3; 2 Cor. iv. 4; Col. i. 15; ii. 17; and the proverb, 'Coming
events cast their shadow before.'
[3] Heb. viii. 2.   [4] ibid., viii. 5.   [5] ibid., ix. 7, 8, 12, 24.
[6] S. John v. 39.   [7] S. Luke xxiv. 27.   [8] ibid., xxiv. 44.
[9] Cf. Acts ii. 25–32; iii. 18–21; iv. 24–27; Rom. x. 4; 1 Cor. x. 1–4, 11;
Gal. iii. 8; iv. 21–27; 2 Tim. iii. 14–17, etc.

and foretold in the Law;[1] by Abraham and Melchizedek, centuries before the giving of the Law,[2] in the Prophets,[3] and in the Psalms.[4] He quotes these passages from the Old Testament in evidence of the truths which are the main subjects of his Epistle, that is, the true divinity and humanity of our Lord, His High Priesthood and Sacrifice, and His office as Mediator of the New Covenant.

5. *The Relevance and Value of Hebrews to the Christian of To-day*

We may be tempted to ask, 'What relevance and particular value to our time and conditions are to be found in an Epistle addressed to a group of Jewish Christians of the first century in view of a local, historical situation which has long passed away, and filled with Hebrew conceptions and allusions which require some study to fully appreciate?'

The answer is:

(*a*) That the Church has formally decided that this Epistle is to be reckoned as one of the apostolic writings which, being inspired by God Himself Who is its primary Author, is to be received and read as a true record of His mind and will. This decision was arrived at despite long disagreement as to who was the human author of this work, and was no doubt motived by the fact that it contains certain definite dogmatic teaching, especially about our Lord's Priesthood and Sacrifice, which, though taken for granted, and so referred to, in other New Testament writings, is not dealt with in so immediate and magisterial a manner.

(*b*) Although, like other Epistles, notably *Romans*, *Galatians*, *Corinthians*, *Colossians*, and *Thessalonians*, it was written in view of a particular situation, it is concerned to see and meet it in the light of facts and truths which belong to, and proceed from, the eternal order of the

---

[1] Heb. iii. 1–6; vii. 28; viii. 1–4; ix. 6–12, 24–26; xiii. 11.
[2] ibid., v. 10; vi. 13–vii. 1–10.   [3] ibid., viii. 8–12; xi. 37, 38.
[4] ibid., i. 5–13; ii. 6–8, 12, 13; iii. 7–11; v. 5, 6; x. 5–7.

divine counsel and will. Its whole argument rests upon the historical fact that the eternal and unchangeable order of the providence of God has been manifested by, and contained within, the Person of His Son, and is thus shown to be valid and necessary for all time and all men. If much of the argument is supported and illustrated by a certain visible projection in time of that timeless order, such as was the Mosaic Law and worship, it is not wholly dependent upon, nor limited by, it. The essential facts and truths, with the implications which flow from them, are of permanent meaning and value, no less to our time than to the past.

(c) Amongst these truths, three are of especial value in the present time in which they are either denied, ignored, or reduced to such meagre proportions as to carry no meaning or conviction. They are those concerning the Person of Jesus Christ; His office as High Priest of the human race; and His Sacrifice on its behalf. About each of these the Epistle affords further evidence to that given by the rest of the New Testament as to what Christians of the first century believed upon the word of those apostolic teachers from whom they had received the Faith. We may, since we are free beings, hold that Faith to be true or false, but the New Testament leaves us no doubt as to what it was, and there is no valid reason for the assumption that the critics, commentators, and novelists of to-day are more likely to know what that Faith was, and is, than those who drank of its very source, and lived, suffered, and died for it. We may know more of its fullness and implications, be able to express it in more definite theological terms, but not more in the sense that we can revise or alter its integral truth and character, so that little remains but a pale and fading shadow of its unique, divine greatness.

The 'Modernist' Christ, whether of the past or the present, is not the Christ of the New Testament, nor of the Church which for twenty centuries has adored Him Who is

'the Word made flesh,'[1] 'in Whom dwelleth all the fullness
of the Godhead in bodily form,'[2] Who 'is the brightness
of [the Father's] glory, and the express Image of His
Person.'[3]

Further, He is the fulfilment of the whole Judaic
dispensation which only finds its true meaning and purpose in Him Who, in superseding and bringing it to
naught, reveals Himself as being all to which it pointed,
the very substance of which it was but a shadow, the
reality which it but dimly adumbrated, the final Word,
of God's revelation, the broken syllables of which the Law,
and the Prophets and Psalmists had uttered in time past;
the Verb[4] Who alone makes the sentence of history and
of the individual life intelligible and meaningful.

Of no less value is the author's exposition of Christ's
mediatorial, priestly, and sacrificial office at a time when
He is so commonly regarded as no more than one of the
world's great religious teachers, or as a superlatively good
man whose chief claim to our reverence is the Sermon
on the Mount, and His many acts of kindness to others.
For in Hebrews, as in the rest of the New Testament, it
is not the Sermon but the Sacrifice; not the teaching but
the Teacher; not the kindly layman but the divinely-
appointed Priest, the one and only Mediator between God
and man, Whom the writer has to declare to us.

All this will appear in Part One in which the dogmatic
teaching of the Epistle is reviewed, and in the Commentary which follows.

(d) Hebrews has as definitely practical a value for the
Christian, and for the world of to-day, as it had for those
to whom it was first addressed.

It is true that Christians to-day are not likely to be
tempted to embrace Judaism. But there is a very real
temptation, and one to which the merely acquiescent or

---

[1] S. John i. 14.   [2] Col. ii. 9.   [3] Heb. i. 3.
[4] Cf. the Latin, *In principio erat Verbum*, and French, *Au commencement était
le Verbe*, of the first verse of S. John's Gospel.

B

ill-instructed Christian is vulnerable, to be led astray by
adherents of one of the many semi-Christian, and even
anti-Christian, substitutes for the Faith which exist in our
midst. They are not endeavouring to persuade us to
return to a religion which had in its favour the fact that it
had, for its time and place, the authority and sanction of
Almighty God, but to forsake one which He has revealed
and made final for a new one, founded by men claiming
to have had some private revelation, and to be possessed
of a greater and truer knowledge of the meaning of Holy
Scripture than that of the Church which wrote and gave
it to the world as the inspired word of God. To yield
to the irrational and fantastic teachings of these cults,
betrayed by the camouflage of Christian terminology and
sentiments under which their falsities are concealed from
the unthinking, is to commit that sin of apostasy of which
Hebrews speaks so plainly. Nor does it do so alone. Our
Lord Himself bade us beware of false teachers,[1] and His
Apostles repeat His warnings.[2]

There is another fact which places Christians of our
time in a somewhat similar position to that in which the
first readers of Hebrews found themselves. They were
surrounded by those of their own race who believed them
to be the dupes and victims of the preachers of the new
religion which they had embraced. The current, popular
thought of their neighbours was set against them. So
Christians to-day find themselves surrounded by an increasing number of men and women who regard them as
adherents of a dying superstition which is already so
moribund that it is hardly worth more than a mild and
pitying tolerance. There is no persecution, though the
possibility of persecution is neither so remote nor so un-
thinkable as some imagine it to be; but the current mood
of the time is set away from Christ and His Church.

[1] S. Matt. vii. 15; S. Mark xiii. 21, 22.
[2] Gal. i. 6–12; Col. ii. 8; 2 Thess. ii. 15; 1 Tim. i, 6, 7, 19; vi. 3–5; 2 Tim.
iii. 6–17; iv. 3, 4; 2 S. Pet. ii. 1–3; iii. 16; 1 S. John ii. 18, 19; iv. 1–3; 2 S.
John 7–11; S. Jude 4, 17–19.

Such a situation often causes doubt and despondency instead of that renewing of faith, confidence, patience, and courage which the author of Hebrews endeavours to re-awaken in his readers. Time has not robbed his words of their strong faith and encouragement, since they are rooted in Him Who is the 'Author and Perfecter' of that faith, even 'Jesus Christ, the Same, yesterday, and to-day, and for ever.'

6. *Plan of the Epistle*

Hebrews is a reasoned treatise in the form of an epistle, in the course of which are passages of fervent exhortation, warning, and encouragement. The author himself calls it a 'word of exhortation.'[1] The main theme is that Jesus Christ, in His Person, His Priesthood, and His Sacrifice, is altogether and uniquely above all the mediators, angels, prophets, and leaders of the Old Covenant, which He has come to fulfil,[2] and in fulfilling, to abrogate and bring to an end.

The Epistle has two well-defined parts:

(1) Chapters i–x. 17. Christ, God-Man, our High Priest and Sacrifice, Mediator of the New Covenant between God and man.

(2) Chapters x. 18–end. Exhortation to persevere in the way which He has dedicated for us.

ANALYSIS

(1) i. Christ, as Son of God, is incomparably and uniquely superior to the prophets and to the angels.

ii. 1–4. Exhortation to give heed to the divine revelation of salvation made in Christ.

ii. 5–18. Christ is God's Son made man, sharer in our flesh and blood, in order that He may be a merciful and faithful High Priest on our behalf.

iii. 1–6. He is worthy of more honour than Moses who

---

[1] Heb. xiii. 22.   [2] Cf. S. Matt. v. 17.

was but a servant in God's house, whereas Christ is Son over His house.

iii. 7–iv. Exhortation not to fall into unbelief, as did the Israelites in the wilderness, lest they should fail to enter into the sabbath rest of God.

v. 1–10. Comparison between the Aaronic priesthood and that of Jesus, priest for ever after the order of Melchizedek.

v. 11–vi. 12. The recipients of the Epistle have failed in making progress in the understanding of the Faith. They must press on to perfection. They are reminded of the deadly character of the sin of apostasy. But their past faith and love give the writer confidence in them.

vi. 13–20. God's promise to Abraham and his seed confirmed by an oath, and fulfilled in Christ, is a strong encouragement to them.

vii. Further comparison between our Lord's priesthood of the order of Melchizedek and that of the Levitical priesthood, which was but temporary and perfected nothing.

viii. Christ has a more excellent ministry than that of the Jewish priests, inasmuch as He is a minister of the true tabernacle in heaven, of which that of the Law was but a copy and shadow.

ix. Comparison of the sacrificial office of the Levitical priesthood with that of Christ, Whose one Sacrifice of Himself has obtained eternal redemption and cleansing from sin. The Old Covenant was ratified by the shedding of the blood of animals, the New one, of which Christ is the Mediator, by His own blood. Having once suffered, He has entered heaven itself, to appear before God for us, from whence He will appear again, unto salvation of them that wait for Him.

x. 1–18. The writer returns to the subject of the inefficiency of the sacrifices of the Old Covenant, now taken away and superseded by the one Sacrifice of Christ.

(2) x. 19–39. Let them, then, have boldness to persevere
in the Faith, by which they may enter into heaven, by
the new and living way which Jesus has dedicated for
them. They are called to a more diligent practice of
their Christian obligations, and warned of the judgement which awaits those who sin wilfully by forsaking
the truth which they have come to know. Let them
remember how well they began, how they have suffered
for that truth, and exercise faith and patience that they
may receive the promise of God.

xi. Let them consider what faith is and does, and the
example of the heroic lives and sufferings of the saints
of old who lived by faith.

xii. Encouraged by so great a cloud of witnesses, let them
lay aside everything which would hinder them in running the race that is set before them, their gaze fixed
upon Jesus, Author and Perfecter of faith. If they
suffer and are chastened, is it not because God treats
them as sons, for their profit, that they may be partakers of His holiness, without which no man shall see
the Lord? They have not come to the dreadful Mount
of Sinai, but to the true and eternal Zion, the city of
the living God, the Church of the firstborn. Let them
not refuse to hear Him Whose blood speaketh better
things than that of Abel.

xiii. The Epistle ends with a series of exhortations concerning Christian virtues and practice, a request for
prayer, a blessing, and some salutations.

PART ONE

THE DOGMATIC TEACHING OF HEBREWS

THE supreme and central figure of the Epistle is Jesus Christ, the eternal Son of God made man, the Mediator of the New Covenant, High Priest of our humanity, the Sacrifice of our redemption. From beginning to end He dominates every page, is the fount and centre of the whole argument, One Who, 'glorious in His apparel,'[1] contains within Himself, and fulfils, the bygone glory of the Old Covenant, as, no less, He holds the future in His hands, He Who is 'the Same, yesterday, and to-day, and for ever.'[2] Timeless, He appears in time; eternal, reigns in heavenly splendour, at once Priest and Victim, Worship and Worshipper, Head and Representative of our race whose nature He embraces that He may clothe it with His own glory.[3] Knowing how little his readers had grown 'in grace and in the knowledge of our Lord and Saviour Jesus Christ,'[4] in which knowledge is eternal life,[5] our author bids them consider (a favourite word of his) the high dignity and significance of the Person and office of Him Whom they are tempted to renounce.

1. He is the Son of God 'Whom He appointed heir of all things, through Whom also He made the worlds,'[6] 'the effulgence of His glory, and the very image of His substance,'[7] Who has been exalted to 'the right hand of the Majesty on high,'[8] Whose Name is more excellent

---

[1] Isa. lxiii. 1. [2] Heb. xiii. 8. [3] ibid., ii. 10; S. John xvii. 22.
[4] 2 S. Pet. iii. 18. [5] S. John xvii. 3.
[6] Heb. i. 2; cf. S. John i. 3; Rom. i. 1–4; Col. i. 16, etc.
[7] Heb. i. 3; cf. S. John xvii. 5, 22; S. Jas. ii. 1; 2 Cor. iv. 6; iv. 4; Col. i. 15.
[8] Heb. i. 3; iv. 14; vi. 19, 20; vii. 27; viii. 1; ix. 12, 24; x. 12, 19, 20; xii. 2.

than that of angels who are bidden to render Him worship, Him of Whom it is said, 'Thy throne, O God, is for
ever and ever . . .' And,

> Thou, Lord, in the beginning, hast laid the
>   foundation of the earth,
> And the heavens are the works of Thy hands:
> They shall perish; but Thou continuest:
> They shall all wax old as doth a garment;
> And as a mantle shalt Thou roll them up,
> As a garment, and they shall be changed:
> But Thou art the same,
> And Thy years shall not fail.

Compared with this august Figure, none other than that of
the Word 'Who was with God, and the Word was God,' of
S. John's Prologue, what are the angels but His ministers,
'sent forth to do service for the sake of them that shall
inherit salvation'?[1] Through them, indeed, had not the
Law been given to Moses?[2] yet was there a greater salvation 'spoken through the Lord,' and borne witness to by
God 'both by signs and wonders, and by manifold powers,
and by gifts of the Holy Ghost, according to His will'?[3]

So also was Jesus 'counted worthy of more glory than
Moses,' who 'indeed was faithful in the house of God as a
servant . . . but Christ as a Son over His house,' whose
builder and maker was God, 'which house we are.'[4]

Greater than angels, than Moses, than the Law, 'for
the Law appointed men high priests, having infirmity;
but the word of the oath [of God], which was after the
Law, appointeth a Son, perfected for evermore,'[5] Who
'hath obtained a ministry the more excellent, by how
much also He is the Mediator of a better covenant, which
hath been enacted upon better promises.'[6] We must
realize with what force all this would fall upon the minds
of Jews to Whom the Mosaic Law, for which their fathers

[1] Heb. i. 14.
[2] Gal. iii. 19; Acts vii. 53; Heb. ii. 2.
[3] Heb. ii. 3, 4.
[4] ibid., iii. 3, 6.
[5] ibid., vii. 28.
[6] ibid., viii. 6.

had suffered and died,[1] had for centuries been sacrosanct, inviolable, unalterable.

Thus at the outset does the writer assert, in common with the rest of the New Testament, the divine Personality of Him with Whom all that follows is concerned. And rightly does he do so since on no other ground could he justify the claims he makes for Jesus as the Mediator of that New Covenant which abrogates the divinely ordained one of the Jewish dispensation, the High Priest 'after the order of Melchizedek,' not of Aaron and the Levitical priesthood, the one Sacrifice which effects all that the ancient sacrifices of Hebrew worship were incapable of doing.

Jesus, then, is the eternal Son of God in a unique and singular sense; Son by nature, 'of one substance' with the Father. But no less is He truly Man, and it is as clothed in our nature, partaker of our flesh and blood,[2] 'in all things made like unto His brethren,'[3] 'touched with the feeling of our infirmities . . . in all points tempted like as we are,'[4] 'Who in the days of His flesh,'[5] was 'made a little lower than the angels,' that we behold Him 'for Whom are all things, and through Whom are all things,' enduring suffering and death on behalf of His brethren, that He might bring 'many sons unto glory.'[6] It was in this human nature, prepared for the divine Word when He was about to come into the world,[7] that the will and purpose of the Father, freely accepted by His Son, was to be fulfilled:

> Then said I, Lo, I come
> (In the roll of the book it is written of Me)
> To do Thy will, O God.

'By which will we have been sanctified through the offering of the Body of Jesus Christ once for all.'[8]

[1] Heb., cf. xi.   [2] ibid., ii. 14.   [3] ibid., ii. 17.
[4] ibid., iv. 15.   [5] ibid., v. 7.   [6] ibid., ii. 9–18.
              [7] ibid. x. 5.   [8] ibid., x. 7–10.

Thus the teaching of this Epistle concerning the Person of our Lord and His Incarnation is stated as plainly and unequivocally as by S. John's 'The Word was made flesh,' and S. Paul's 'In Him dwelleth all the fullness of the Godhead bodily.'[1]

2. From the consideration of this fundamental fact and doctrine we pass to that of our Lord's mission.

(a) He is the bearer of God's final and complete revelation of Himself and His will to man. Nay, He *is* that revelation, the Truth itself, of old time made known in part, and in various ways, but now manifested openly and fully, the divine Word translated into our language in the Incarnate Son of God.[2] In the words of S. John of the Cross, 'In giving us, as He did, His Son, Who is His Word —and He has no other—He spake to us altogether, once and for all, in this single Word, and He has no occasion to speak further.'[3] Jesus is 'the Apostle and High Priest of our confession,'[4] by Whom the divine will has been proclaimed on earth, which, 'having at the first been spoken through the Lord, was confirmed unto us by them that heard.'[5] He is 'the Author and Perfecter of faith,'[6] by which we live, Whose words 'shall not pass away.'[7]

(b) He is the one 'Mediator of the New Covenant,'[8] 'the surety of a better covenant,'[9] one promised by God through His prophet Jeremiah,[10] and containing the substance and reality of which the Old Covenant was but a figure and type, a shadow cast before of 'good things to come.'[11]

(c) He is 'the High Priest of our confession,'[12] 'a merciful and faithful High Priest in things pertaining to God,'[13] 'named of God a High Priest after the order of Melchizedek,'[14] 'made not after the law of a carnal commandment,

[1] Col. ii. 9.   [2] Heb. i. 1, 2.   [3] *Ascent*, Bk. II, xxii. 3.
[4] Heb. iii. 1.   [5] ibid., ii. 3.   [6] ibid., xii. 2.
[7] S. Luke xxi. 33.   [8] Heb. ix. 14; xii. 24.   [9] ibid., vii. 22; cf. viii. 6.
[10] Jer. xxxi. 31–34; Heb. viii. 8–12.   [11] Heb. ix. 11; x. 1.
[12] ibid. iii. 1.   [13] ibid., ii. 17.   [14] ibid. v. 10; vi. 20.

but after the power of an endless life,'[1] Who, unlike those
of the Aaronic priesthood, whose office was brought to an
end through death, 'hath His priesthood unchangeable.'[2]

(d) Unlike the priests of the Old Covenant, who offered
sacrifices in place of themselves, and that daily, Jesus is
not only Priest and Offerer, but also Victim and Offering,
He of Whom it had been said to Abraham, 'God will
provide Himself a lamb for a burnt-offering,'[3] and of
Whose Sacrifice Isaiah had spoken in time past.[4] He
'needeth not daily, like those high priests, to offer up
sacrifices, first for His own sins, and then for the sins of
the people: for this He did once for all, when He offered
up Himself.'[5] 'Christ having come a high priest of good
things to come, through the greater and more perfect
tabernacle, not made with hands, that is to say, not of this
creation, nor yet by the blood of goats and calves, but
through His own blood, entered in once for all into the
holy place, having obtained eternal redemption,'[6] 'by the
sacrifice of Himself.'[7] We are sanctified through the offering of the body of Christ once for all,[8] 'one sacrifice for
sins,'[9] by which we have 'boldness to enter into the
holy place by the blood of Jesus, by the way which He
dedicated for us, a new and living way, through the veil,
that is to say, His flesh.'[10] We are come to 'the blood of
sprinkling which speaketh better things than that of Abel,'[11]
even 'the blood of the eternal covenant,'[12] of 'the Lamb
slain from the foundation of the world.'[13]

This whole conception of the need of priesthood and
sacrifice is so foreign, even to many professing Christians
of modern times, that some consideration must be given
to it. That it is so foreign is due to such facts as those of
the failure to recognize the vast difference which exists
between the Creator and the creature, of man's depen-

[1] Heb. vii. 17.   [2] ibid., vii. 23, 24.   [3] Gen. xxii. 8.
[4] Isa. liii.   [5] Heb. vii. 27.   [6] ibid., ix. 11.
[7] ibid., ix. 27.   [8] ibid., x. 10.   [9] ibid., x. 12.
[10] ibid., x. 19, 20.   [11] ibid., xii. 24.   [12] ibid., xiii. 20.
                           [13] Rev. xiii. 8.

dence upon God, of his obligations toward God, worship, love, service, and of the fact of sin which makes it impossible for man to render to God that to which He has a right as God. Both Holy Scripture and human history show that these were the sources of the beginnings and development of priesthood and sacrifice which were not imposed upon men from without, but sprang from within man's inner nature which, created in the image of God, and illumined thereby, recognized its creaturely condition, and its essential need to express itself in the worship, love, and service of the Supreme Being. Only in periods of a high material civilization, like that of Rome in the latter days of the Empire, or that of to-day, have men lost the sense of God, and of their relation to Him, only to find that they could not divest themselves of that inner imperative of their nature which, when God is denied or ignored, compels them to worship and serve gods of their own devising . . . to their ruin.

Men are not merely individuals, they are members of society, and whilst it has always been recognized that as an individual a man could approach God directly, yet as a social being he should unite himself with his fellows in acts of corporate worship. Such worship, whether private or communal, is man's offering of himself, with all that he is and has, to God, from Whom he confesses he has received all, and to Whom he owes all. In both cases he has ever felt that such an offering should be expressed by some outward act which should symbolize it. So, whether in private or public worship, he presents some material gift to God as a sacrifice by which he openly acknowledges the right of God to claim his whole devotion and service. But when such an act is performed in common with other members of the family, tribe, or nation, then one man, the father, the headman, the king, and, later, the priest, is chosen to act, to offer the sacrifice in the name of the whole community.

All this, we repeat, arose from, and was determined by,

man's nature, was the spontaneous and universal expression of that nature, not something imposed upon it, as has been alleged, by a priestly caste trading upon the ignorance and superstition of their fellows.

Man's experience of the fact of sin and its consequences added another note to his conception of sacrifice. For by sin he had, to greater or less extent, renounced God, asserted his independence of Him, violated His will, and become unworthy of approaching Him in worship. So his sacrifice becomes one of penitence, propitiation, reparation. By his sin man has refused to surrender his life to God, has incurred the penalty of both physical and spiritual death. So sacrifice, whilst retaining its primary meaning, becomes an atonement for sin, in which the death of the victim symbolizes the death to sin of the offerer, the blood of the victim signifying the life of the offerer.

The sense of separation from God which sin has evoked, and of the sinner's unworthiness, enhances the position of the priest whose office entitles him to enter the divine presence and offer the sacrifice on behalf of the sinful man or community. To be a priest is to be a mediator, 'he is appointed for men in things pertaining to God, that he may offer both gifts and sacrifices for sins.'[1] As a mediator, he stands between God and sinful humanity, in order that, as its representative, he may restore that relation to God which sin has broken.

Such was the priest of the Hebrew covenant, one of a specially chosen tribe, that of Levi, to which alone the exercise of the priesthood had been committed by God. But that priesthood, like the covenant which it served, was a provisional, temporary one, 'imposed until a time of reformation,'[2] which could not do more than signify and prefigure the inauguration of a new covenant, priesthood, and sacrifice by which, in the Person of His Son, God should abrogate that of old, establishing in its

[1] Heb. v. 1.   [2] ibid., ix. 10.

place the new, universal, eternal covenant, priesthood, and sacrifice of Jesus Christ, 'named of God a High Priest after the order of Melchizedek.'[1] The Levitical priesthood, and so the Law,[2] is abolished 'because of its weakness and unprofitableness, for the Law made nothing perfect,'[3] 'for it is impossible that the blood of bulls and goats should take away sins,'[4] much less 'make the worshipper perfect.'[5]

But this abolition does not mean that the need for priesthood and sacrifice no longer exists. On the contrary, Jesus 'taketh away the first that He may establish the second,'[6] His own divine-human priesthood, and His 'one Sacrifice for sins for ever.'[7] Henceforth there is no other sacrifice, no other priesthood save that of Christ Himself, Priest and Victim for ever, Who, having once for all offered the Sacrifice of Himself upon the Cross, entered 'into heaven itself, now to appear before the face of God for us,'[8] the Lamb 'standing, as though it had been slain.'[9]

But if this be so, how may we speak of a Christian order of priesthood, and of the Eucharist as a Sacrifice, as the Church has done from the earliest days, and this with the Epistle to the Hebrews in her hands? How can we justify the implication that Christ has not only established His Sacrifice in heaven but also on earth? Does not the author of Hebrews make a clear distinction between repeated sacrifices offered daily, which have been brought to an end, and the one Sacrifice of Christ Who needs not 'that He should offer Himself often'?[10]

Let the last question be answered by saying that the writer is referring to the sacrifices of the Old Law only; his mind is entirely on the past, not on the present or future. He was well aware that the principal, and indeed

[1] ibid., v. 10.   [2] ibid., vii. 12.   [3] ibid., vii. 18, 19.
[4] ibid., x. 4.   [5] ibid., ix. 9.   [6] ibid., x. 9.
[7] ibid., x. 12.   [8] ibid., ix. 24.   [9] Rev. v. 6.
[10] Heb. ix. 25; cf. x. 11–13.

only, Christian act of worship of his time was the Eucharist, to which he seems to refer when he writes, 'We have
an altar, whereof they have no right to eat which serve
the tabernacle,'[1] and does certainly refer when he bids
his readers not to 'forsake the gathering of' themselves
together.[2]

With regard to the question of a divinely ordained order
of priesthood in the Church as distinct from the priesthood
of all Christians, and carrying with it functions which are
peculiar to it, we may ask first by virtue of what right does
any man name himself Christian, and believe that as such
Christ has made him to be a priest 'unto God and
Father'?[3] By no other right than that of his being united
to Christ, made a member of His mystical Body, a branch
of the true Vine, a sharer in, and a continuer of, the office
and mission of Christ, as the whole of the New Testament
teaches. And, secondly, is it not equally clear from the
New Testament that Christ chose, and conferred upon
His Apostles, certain powers, with authority to exercise
them in His Name?[4] The Acts and Epistles show that the
Apostles not only exercised these powers, which bore a
priestly character, and were not confined merely to
preaching the Gospel, but also provided for the extended
and continued exercise of them by conferring them upon
others.[5]

There is, then, a Christian priesthood ordained to perpetuate the one priesthood of Christ upon earth, not one
which adds anything to His, or takes its place, but is *His*
priesthood conferred upon, and shared in by, those whom
His Church recognizes as having been chosen by Him
to this high vocation.

And as there is a Christian priesthood wholly dependent
upon, and derived from, that of Christ, the priest acting

[1] Heb. xiii. 10.   [2] ibid., x. 25.   [3] Rev. i. 6.
[4] Cf. S. Matt. x. 1–14; xvi. 13–19; xxviii. 16–20; S. Luke xxii. 19, 20;
S. John xv. 16, 26; xvi. 13; xvii. 6–9; xx. 21–23.
[5] Acts i. 21–26; ii. 41; viii. 14–18; xiii. 1–3; xix. 1–7; 1 Cor. xi. 23–26;
2 Cor. ii. 10; v. 18, 19; 1 Tim. iv. 14; 2 Tim. i. 6; Titus i. 5.

in and through His Body, the Church, so there is a Christian sacrifice, even that foretold by the last prophet of the Old Covenant,[1] instituted by our Lord Himself,[2] and offered daily in His Church until He come again.

How can this statement be justified in view of the insistence of Hebrews that Christ offered His Sacrifice once for all on Calvary, and ascended into heaven as our High Priest and Sacrifice where 'He ever liveth to make intercession for us'?[3] We have noted already that the writer is dealing only with the abrogation of the sacrifices of the Old Covenant, and this on the ground that they could not take away sins,[4] or 'make the worshipper perfect.'[5] His words have no reference to the Christian doctrine that the Eucharistic Sacrifice, because of what it is, does take away sin and perfect the worshipper, as the prayers of the Liturgy constantly repeat. Before elucidating this doctrine, attention must be given to a fact scarcely, if ever, recognized by non-Catholics, that is, that the celebration of the Eucharist as the foremost and regular act of Christian worship preceded the writing of the New Testament documents, and was not a consequence of what is read there concerning it. It existed independently of the New Testament Scriptures, resting solely upon the apostolic account of its institution by our Lord, such as S. Paul mentions as well known,[6] and speaks of as a rite familiar to his readers in which they 'proclaim the Lord's death until He come.' There was, then, from the earliest days of the Faith the recognition of a real link and purpose between the Sacrifice of Calvary and the Eucharistic offering. What was, and is, that link and purpose? It is that what Jesus did at the Last Supper on Maundy Thursday night, what He did on the Cross, and what is done, at His command, in the Eucharist, are, despite all outward and temporary conditions, *one and the same act.*

---

[1] Mal. i. 11.
[2] S. Luke xxii. 19, 20; 1 Cor. xi. 23–26.
[3] Heb. vii. 25.
[4] ibid., x. 4, 12.
[5] ibid., ix. 10.
[6] 1 Cor. xi. 23–26; cf. x. 15, 16.

The Passion of our Lord begins with His oblation of Himself in the upper room, 'This is My Body which is given for you: this do in remembrance of Me. . . . This cup is the New Covenant in My Blood, even that which is poured out for you.'[1] It is continued, one unbroken act, in His public offering, the immolation of Himself, upon the Cross. In the upper room He acts primarily as Priest, on Calvary, as the Victim, in Whose death the Sacrifice, already consecrated, is consummated. At the Resurrection He enters into His glory (the Ascension being the outward manifestation of the accomplished fact of the Father's acceptance of His Sacrifice, and of His now permanent retention of that human body in which He had offered that Sacrifice), to be for ever the Priest and Victim of humanity.

There cannot be any other sacrifice than His which, once offered, He now presents in Person for ever in heaven. Note, we say, presents, for there is no offering there such as was once for all made on the Cross. 'Christ being raised from the dead, dieth no more; death hath no more dominion over Him. For in that He died, He died unto sin once: but the life that He liveth, He liveth unto God,'[2] lives as the eternal Priest and Victim, Sacrifice and Altar, of our salvation.

The sacrifice of the Eucharist is the Sacrifice, no other, of which Jesus made oblation at the Last Supper, which He offered upon the Cross, and which He presents in heaven. The same, because both Priest and Victim are the same, He Whose Sacrifice consummated in time, but not limited either to time, or by spatial conditions, remains eternal, so that, in the Eucharist there is no question of His being made a Victim, for that He is, but only of our acceptance, and our offering of His Sacrifice as *our* Sacrifice, and this in the sacramental, symbolic (but real) manner which He commanded us *to do*, not merely to

[1] S. Luke xxii. 19, 20; cf. 1 Cor. xi. 24–26.   [2] Rom. vi. 9, 10.

think of or talk of or sing about. According to S. Paul, it is not by preaching only, but by the offering and partaking of the Eucharistic Sacrifice that we 'proclaim the Lord's death until He come.'[1]

He commanded us to do what He had done for us in order that we might effectually share in His Sacrifice by making it ours. For, amongst other differences between Calvary and the altar is this, that on the Cross Jesus offered Himself as the Sacrifice of our redemption, whereas in the Eucharist it is His mystical Body, the Church, which does so.

> What He did at Supper seated,
> Christ ordained to be repeated.
> His memorial ne'er to cease;
> And, His word for guidance taking,
> Bread and wine we hallow, making
> Thus our Sacrifice of peace.

So wrote the greatest theologian of the mediaeval age, expressing in incomparable verse what the Church had believed from the beginning. So, too, does a modern writer, William Bright.

> And now, O Father, mindful of the love
> That bought us, once for all, on Calvary's Tree,
> And having with us Him that pleads above,
> We here present, we here spread forth to Thee
> That only Offering perfect in Thine eyes,
> The one true, pure, immortal Sacrifice.

3. Joined to the outstanding truths of the Personality and Mission of Jesus, the writer has much to say of His character, and more than any one else, except the Evangelists, of His human life. One of our race, 'He is not ashamed to call us' His brethren;[2] and His personal experience of our infirmities and temptations invites us 'to draw near with boldness unto the throne of grace, that

---

[1] I Cor. xi. 26.   [2] Heb. ii. 12; cf. S. Luke viii. 21.

C

we may receive mercy, and may find grace to help us in time of need.'[1] 'Holy, guileless, undefiled, separated from sinners,' and in His human nature 'made higher than the heavens,'[2] He yet bids us 'draw near with a true heart in fullness of faith . . . for He is faithful that promised,'[3] He 'the great Shepherd of the sheep' through Whom God wills 'to work in us that which is well-pleasing in His sight,' and to make us 'perfect in every good thing to do His will.'[4] He has accomplished the mission for which He came into the world;[5] has endured temptation,[6] 'yet without sin';[7] has exhibited a profound trust in God His Father;[8] has been faithful to His priestly office,[9] and to God Who 'appointed Him Son over His own house';[10] and 'though He was a Son, yet learned obedience by the things which He suffered.'[11]

Of His human life, we read of His descent from the tribe of Judah;[12] of His growth in perfection;[13] of the 'signs and wonders' which attested the divine character of His mission;[14] of His prayer and suffering;[15] His crucifixion.[16] His Resurrection is only mentioned once,[17] but is implied in many of the passages in which the writer dwells on His Ascension to, and abiding session in, our human nature at the right hand of the Father in heaven. It is the Incarnate Son Who is thus 'crowned with glory and worship,'[18] Who has 'passed into the heavens,'[19] having been saved from death;[20] Who is 'set down on the right hand of the throne of the Majesty in the heavens,'[21] and this in the veil of His flesh,[22] in which He became, and remains for ever, our High Priest and Representative 'Who ever liveth to make intercession for us,'[23] until that day when He 'shall appear

---

[1] Heb. iv. 15, 16.   [2] ibid. vii. 26, 27.   [3] ibid., x. 22.
[4] ibid., xiii. 20, 21.   [5] Cf. S. John xvii. 4.   [6] Heb. ii. 15.
[7] ibid., iv. 15.   [8] ibid., ii. 13.   [9] ibid., ii. 17.
[10] ibid., iii. 6.   [11] ibid., v. 8.   [12] ibid., vii. 14.
[13] ibid., ii. 10; v. 9.   [14] ibid., ii. 4.   [15] ibid., ii. 9, 14; v. 7; xii. 2, 3.
[16] ibid., xiii. 12.   [17] ibid., xiii. 20.   [18] ibid., ii. 9.
[19] ibid., iv. 14.   [20] ibid., v. 7.   [21] ibid. viii. 1; ix. 12, 24; x. 12.
[22] ibid., x. 20.   [23] ibid., vii. 25.

a second time, apart from sin, to them that wait for Him, unto salvation.'[1]

4. The supreme object and end of His Incarnation and Passion, of His priestly and sacrificial office, is to 'bring to nought him that had the power of death, that is, the devil; and to deliver all them who through fear of death were all their life subject to bondage.'[2] This He did by His Sacrifice upon Calvary, by which He 'obtained eternal redemption' for us by the offering of 'the blood of Christ, Who through the eternal Spirit offered Himself without blemish unto God,'[3] and 'became unto all them that obey Him the cause of eternal salvation.'[4]

5. The divinity of the Holy Ghost is implied, and mention made of some aspects of His office. God has borne witness to the preaching of the Gospel 'by gifts of the Holy Ghost,'[5] Who has spoken through the Scriptures of the Old Testament,[6] and by the entry of the high priest alone into the Holy of holies, once in the year, signified 'that the way into the holy place hath not yet been made manifest, whilst as the first tabernacle was still standing.'[7] The offering of the blood of Christ on our behalf was made 'through the eternal Spirit';[8] 'the Spirit of grace'[9] of Whom Christians have been 'made partakers.'[10]

6. Christian life and practice. The author and source of the Christian, spiritual, life is Jesus Christ, 'the Apostle and High Priest of our confession'[11] 'Whose house we are,'[12] of Whom 'we are become partakers,'[13] Who 'became unto all that obey Him the author of eternal salvation';[14] Who 'is able to save to the uttermost them that draw nigh unto God through Him';[15] having entered 'into heaven itself, now to appear before the face of God for us.'[16] He is the 'Author and Perfecter' of that faith by which we

---

[1] ibid., ix. 28.
[2] ibid., ii. 14, 15.
[3] ibid., ix. 11–14.
[4] ibid., v. 9.
[5] ibid., ii. 4.
[6] ibid., iii. 7; x. 15.
[7] ibid., ix. 7–9.
[8] ibid., ix. 14.
[9] ibid., x. 30.
[10] ibid., vi. 4.
[11] ibid., iii. 1.
[12] ibid., iii. 6.
[13] ibid., iii. 14.
[14] ibid., v. 9.
[15] ibid., vii. 25.
[16] ibid., ix. 24.

accept the Gospel which He taught, from the lips of those
who, having heard it, proclaimed it to men.[1] To be a
Christian is to be one who has been 'enlightened' in
Baptism,[2] 'and tasted of the heavenly gift,' made partaker
of the Holy Ghost, 'and tasted the good word of God, and
the powers of the age to come';[3] who is within the 'New
Covenant' promised of God through Jeremiah;[4] has been
'sanctified through the offering of the Body of Jesus Christ
once for all';[5] so to be treated by God as a son;[6] to have
received 'a kingdom which cannot be shaken';[7] to have
'come unto Mount Zion, and unto the city of the living
God, the heavenly Jerusalem, and to innumerable hosts
of angels, to the general assembly and church of the firstborn who are enrolled in heaven, and to God the Judge
of all, and to the spirits of just men made perfect, and to
Jesus the mediator of a new covenant, and to the blood
of sprinkling that speaketh better than that of Abel,'[8] to
have 'an altar, whereof they have no right to eat which
serve the tabernacle.'[9]

The Epistle is full of the conception of the Christian
life as a progress toward perfection. Of our Lord Himself
we read that God willed 'in bringing many sons to glory,
to make the author of their salvation perfect through
sufferings.'[10]

The need for a New Covenant lay in the fact that 'the
Law made nothing perfect,'[11] for if there was perfection
through the Levitical priesthood (for under it hath the
people received the Law) what further need was that
another priest should arise after the order of Melchizedek?[12]
'For the Law having a shadow of the good things to come,
not the very image of the things, they can never with the
same sacrifices year by year, which they offer continually,
make perfect them that draw nigh . . . for it is impossible

---

[1] Heb. ii. 3.   [2] Cf. ibid., x. 32.   [3] ibid., vi. 4, 5.
[4] Jer. xxxi. 31–34.   [5] Heb. x. 10.   [6] ibid., xii. 7.
[7] ibid., xii. 28.   [8] ibid., xii. 22–24.   [9] ibid., xiii. 10.
[10] ibid., ii. 10; cf. v. 9; vii. 28.   [11] ibid., vii. 19; cf. ix. 9, 10.
[12] ibid., vii. 11; viii. 6, 7.

that the blood of bulls and goats should take away sins.'[1] But Jesus 'by one offering . . . hath perfected for ever them that are sanctified.'[2] It is His mission to take away the first Covenant, that He may establish the second.[3] He 'having come a high priest of the good things to come, through the greater and more perfect tabernacle,' that is, of His human nature which was 'not made with hands, that is to say, not of this creation,'[4] but was 'conceived by the Holy Ghost' in the womb of Mary, and of which it is said, 'a body didst Thou prepare for Me,'[5] and later is called 'the veil, that is to say, His flesh,' the 'new and living way which He hath dedicated for us.'[6]

The Epistle insists upon, and underlines, the truth that human life has an end, not in the sense of a full stop, a conclusion, but a consummation, a perfecting of our human nature by its union with God Who is its perfecting end and fulfilment. Life has a meaning, a purpose, a goal to be sought and attained, a perfection to be realized. This, the ancient Law, the Old Covenant, the Levitical priesthood and sacrifices pointed to, and were a type or figure of,[7] 'a copy and shadow of heavenly things,'[8] could not either fully reveal or enable men to accomplish. But now God had spoken in the Person of His Son in Whom both man's end and the way thereto had been made known, deliverance from the power of sin and death effected and proclaimed, by the bringing in of 'a better hope,'[9] 'both sure and steadfast,'[10] the confession of which must be held fast that it waver not,[11] since, with faith and charity, it unites us to Christ, 'if we hold fast the beginning of our confidence firm unto the end.'[12]

Now, the Jewish Christians to whom the Epistle was written had received the Gospel which 'having at the first been spoken through the Lord, was confirmed unto

---

[1] ibid., x. 1–4.   [2] ibid., x. 14.   [3] ibid., x. 9.   [4] ibid., ix. 11.
[5] ibid., x. 5.   [6] ibid., x. 19, 20; cf. S. John ii. 21.   [7] Heb. ix. 8, 9.
[8] ibid., viii. 5.   [9] ibid., vii. 19.   [10] ibid., vi. 19.
[11] ibid., iii. 6; vi. 11; x. 23.   [12] ibid., iii. 6, 14.

us by them that heard.'[1] They had accepted, though with
slight understanding, 'the first principles of Christ . . .
repentance from dead works, and of faith towards God,
of the teaching of baptisms, and of laying on of hands,
and of resurrection of the dead, and of eternal judgement.'[2]
But they had not learnt that unless they grew up in
understanding, passing from the childhood to the adult
stage of the Christian life, they could not hope to preserve
what they had received. The Faith can be held only as
one progresses in knowledge and love. The milk of the
word of God must be followed by 'the solid food' of full-
grown men, 'even those who by reason of use have their
senses exercised to discern good and evil.'[3] The lack of
such progress has brought about the danger of 'falling
away from the living God,' of becoming 'hardened by the
deceitfulness of sin,' and of that disobedience by which
their fathers provoked God in the wilderness.[4]

Their need is 'to press on to perfection,'[5] to renew the
diligence they had once shown 'unto the full assurance
of hope even to the end';[6] 'to draw near with a true heart
in fullness of faith,' holding fast the confession of their
hope that it waver not;[7] and running 'with patience the
race that is set before them, looking unto Jesus, the
Author and Perfecter of faith' and encouraged by the
'great cloud of witnesses'[8] who 'all died in faith, not having
received the promises, but having seen them and greeted
them from afar.'[9] 'God having some better thing concerning us [Christians], that apart from us they should
not be made perfect.'[10]

The writer exhorts his readers to practise the virtues of
faith,[11] of which he gives examples from the past in
chapter xi, of hope,[12] of charity;[13] to be diligent[14] and bold[15]

[1] Heb., ii. 3.   [2] ibid., vi. 1, 2.   [3] ibid., v. 11–vi. 2.
[4] ibid., iii. 7–iv. 13.   [5] ibid., vi. 1.   [6] ibid., vi. 10, 11.
[7] ibid., x. 22.   [8] ibid., xii. 1, 2.   [9] ibid., x. 13.
[10] ibid., xi. 40.   [11] ibid., iii. 12; iv. 1, 2; x. 22, 38, 39.
[12] ibid., iii. 6; vi. 18, 19; vii. 19; x. 23.   [13] ibid., vi. 10; x. 24; xiii. 1, 2.
[14] ibid., iv. 11; vi. 11.   [15] ibid., iv. 16; x. 19, 35.

in their approach to God; to 'hold fast the beginning of their confidence,'[1] and 'to press on to perfection,'[2] exercising patience[3] and endurance[4] in that chastening which is for their profit, 'that they may be partakers of His holiness.'

They are not to forsake the assembling of themselves together at the Eucharist, 'as the manner of some is.'[5] That the reference is to the Eucharist, and not to informal gatherings for prayer, etc., is plain from the use of the term 'assembling,'[6] which was not used for the former. Prayer for mercy and 'grace to help in time of need,'[7] and for others, the writer especially,[8] with the offering up of 'a sacrifice of praise to God continually, that is, the fruit of lips which make confession to His Name.' Such praise is to be joined with practical service of their neighbour, 'to do good and communicate [i.e. share with, contribute to] forget not: for with such sacrifices God is well pleased.'[9] They are to remember 'them that had rule over' them, and 'spake unto you the word of God,' and to 'imitate their faith,'[10] and to obey and submit to their present pastors.[11] Marriage is to be held 'in honour among all,' and all impurity forsaken.[12] They are to be 'free from the love of money,' being content with what they have, and trusting in God to supply all their need,[13] and to offer 'service to God with reverence and awe.'[14]

---

[1] ibid., iii. 15.   [2] ibid., vi. 1.   [3] ibid., vi. 12; x. 36; xii. 2.
[4] ibid., xii. 3–11.   [5] ibid., x. 25.   [6] Cf. xii. 23.
[7] ibid., iv. 16.   [8] ibid., xiii. 18, 19.
[9] ibid., xiii. 15, 16; cf. vi. 10, 11; x. 24, 34; xiii. 1–3.
[10] ibid., xiii. 7.   [11] ibid., xiii. 17.   [12] ibid., xiii. 4.
[13] ibid., xiii. 5, 6.   [14] ibid., xii. 28, 29.

PART TWO

INTRODUCTORY NOTE TO COMMENTARY

THE main argument of the Epistle, and its development
and explication, are clearly stated, but there are
several passages to which various commentators, both
ancient and modern, have given different interpretations.
To consider and discuss these would be beyond the purpose of this book which is to provide the ordinary reader
with such aid as shall enable him to understand its teaching and message. The present writer, therefore, having
given consideration to such diversities of interpretation,
has chosen those which seem to be most conformable
to the rest of Holy Scripture, and to the ruling of
S. Thomas Aquinas, 'Disciples can without difficulty take
either side they please when Doctors of Scripture differ—
provided their opinions do not conflict with the faith or
sound morals';[1] and to that of S. Augustine, 'Each one
must consult the Rule of Faith which he has received from
the plainer passages of Scripture, and from the authority
of the Church.'[2]

The reader will find many references to other books of
the Bible in this Commentary, as in the preceding chapters. This is due to the belief of the author that the best
interpretation of Holy Scripture is to be found in the
Bible itself. For although it is composed of books of
diverse character, one single purpose runs through it from
beginning to end, and this cannot be better seen and
understood than by 'reading the Bible biblically,' to
borrow a Dominican phrase.

[1] *Summa Theologica* I, Q. lxviii, art. 1.   [2] *Doctrina Christiana*, iii. 2.

COMMENTARY ON THE TEXT

God, having of old time spoken unto the fathers in the prophets by divers portions and in divers manners, hath at the end of these days spoken unto us in His Son.

The Epistle begins with a statement of the main theme which all that follows is concerned to develop and amplify, that is, the contrast between the old and the new revelation and covenant, and the superiority and finality of the latter as compared with the provisional and temporary character of the former. God Himself is the Author of both: the one, temporary, preparatory, incomplete, designed to educate and train the Hebrew people, chosen to be witness to the one God, and to foreshadow better things to come; the other, complete, perfect, and for all time. This implies, though it is not in the author's purpose to draw attention to it, that there is no foundation for the assertion that the Old Testament picture of God is contrary to that of the New. All teaching must be adapted to the capacities of those who are being taught. The fact that lessons given to the kindergarten and lower forms are simple, elementary, and concrete in character, does not mean that they are contrary to, and contradictory of, those given later to higher forms. They are indeed necessary to the understanding of more advanced lessons. So was it with God's revelation of Himself and His will, since He deals with all His creatures according to their nature, capacity, and need.

'Of old time,' then, God spoke to His people 'in the prophets,' the term being used here, as in other parts of the New Testament, to include such inspired leaders as Abraham, 'for he is a prophet';[1] Moses, 'there arose not a prophet since in Israel like unto Moses';[2] and David, 'being a prophet.'[3]

---

[1] Gen. xx. 7.   [2] Deut. xxxiv. 10; Acts vii. 37.   [3] Acts ii. 30.

'In,' not merely 'through,' the prophets. For they were not passive instruments, like a telephone, or a pen in the hand of a writer, 'whose function,' says S. Thomas, 'is to be acted upon, not to act.' But man is not an instrument of that sort; he is so acted upon by the Holy Spirit that he himself also acts—since he has free will.[1] So writes S. Peter that 'holy men of God spake as they were moved by the Holy Ghost.'[2]

'By divers portions and in divers manners,' that is, at different times, in part, and in various and differing ways, such as dreams, visions, angelic appearances, words, etc.

'At the end of these days.' In the Old Testament this expression is used of the time of Messianic kingdom of God on earth.[3] In the New Testament it has two meanings: when, as here, it stands in contrast to the Old Dispensation, it means the Christian era, including the time in which the author is writing;[4] but when something in the future is spoken of, it means the time immediately before the Second Advent which the Christians of the first century thought was at hand.[5]

Hath spoken to us in His Son, Whom He appointed heir of all things, through Whom also He made the worlds.

The distinction between the Old Testament prophets and Christ is at once made clear. They were mortal men. He is God's eternally-begotten Son, and heir of all; they were creatures, He is the Creator.[6] In the New Testament 'son' and 'heir' are correlatives.[7]

'Whom He appointed.' Already Lord and heir[8] of all things as their Creator, the eternal Son by becoming man became so in time, and as God incarnate accomplished the new creation, the redemption and restoration of all things.[9]

[1] *Sum. Theol.* I–II, Q. lxviii, art. 3, ad. 2.   [2] 2 S. Pet. i. 21.
[3] Gen. xlix. 1; Isa. ii. 2, etc.   [4] Cf. Heb. ix. 26.
[5] Cf. Acts ii. 17; S. Jas. v. 3; 1 S. Pet. i. 20, etc.
[6] S. John i. 3, 10.   [7] Cf. S. Mark xii. 6, 7.
[8] Cf. Ps. ii.   [9] Cf. Rom. viii. 19-23; Rev. xxi. 1, 5.

COMMENTARY ON THE TEXT: I. 2–3

Who being the effulgence of His glory, and the very image of His substance.

The glory of God is all that He is in Himself, which, so far as it was possible for man to perceive, was revealed in Christ. Such a revelation was promised by the prophets,[1] and made visible in our Lord.[2] The Greek word translated 'effulgence' (A.V. 'brightness') means both a ray of light proceeding from a luminous body, as do rays from the sun, and the reflection of the luminous body in some object. Both meanings may be applied to our Lord; the former as in the Nicene Creed, 'Light of Light,' and the latter as it is God Himself Who becomes visible in Christ.[3]

'The very image of His substance,' the impressed image of His essence. The word 'substance' here has a different meaning from that in chapter xi. 1, 'faith is the substance of things hoped for.' Here it stands, as in the Nicene Creed, for the essence and being of God.[4] He is the true and perfect image after which man was created, and by which he is to be renewed,[5] conformed,[6] and changed 'into the same image.'[7] The word here has the same sense as when we say of a child that he is the image of his father or mother.

And upholding all things by the word of His power.

He is not only the Creator of all things, but also continually sustains them in being, and is the final end toward which they are borne. For 'All things have been created through Him, and unto Him; and He is before all things, and in Him all things consist,' that is, are held together in being.[8]

---

[1] Num. xiv. 21; Isa. xxxv. 2; xl. 5; Hab. ii. 14.
[2] 2 Cor. iv. 6, 'the light of the knowledge of the glory of God in the face of Jesus Christ.' Cf. S. John i. 14.
[3] Cf. 2 Cor. v. 19.
[4] Cf. S. John x. 30, 'I and My Father are one'; Col. i. 15, 'Who is the image of the invisible God'; 2 Cor. iv. 4, 'Christ Who is the image of God.'
[5] Col. iii. 10.   [6] Rom. viii. 29.   [7] 2 Cor. iii. 18.
[8] Col. i. 16, 17; Eph. i. 10.

*When He had made purification for sins, sat down on the right
hand of the Majesty on high.*

We pass, in this sentence for a moment, from the plain
assertions of the divine Personality of our Lord to a
passing reference to His humanity, and to His Priesthood
and Sacrifice. For it is by the latter, accomplished in our
nature, that He merited the right to assume, as God-Man,
the position of authority and power in heaven.[1]

*Having become by so much better than the angels, as He hath
inherited a more excellent name than they.*

The writer comes to the special theme of the second half
of this opening section, namely, that the incarnate Christ
is above the angels, having 'a Name which is above every
name.'[2]

For unto which of the angels said He at any time,
  Thou art My Son,
  This day have I begotten Thee?[3]
and again,
  I will be to Him a Father,
  And He shall be to Me a Son?[4]

Son of God from all eternity, in becoming Man He
'was made a little lower than the angels'[5] by taking our
human nature which, in the hierachy of created beings,
ranks below that of the angels, He inherits the name
'Son' as Man. It is as 'Son of Man' that He most

[1] Cf. S. Mark xvi. 19; Acts v. 30, 31; Rom. viii. 34; Phil. ii. 8–11;
Rev. v. 6; etc.; the Preface for the Feast of Christ-King, 'Who didst anoint
Thine only-begotten Son, our Lord Jesus Christ, with the oil of gladness,
to be a priest for ever, and King of the whole world: that offering Himself
an unspotted sacrifice of peace upon the altar of the cross, He might
accomplish the Sacrament of the redemption of mankind: and making all
creatures subject to His governance, might deliver up to Thine infinite
Majesty, an eternal and universal kingdom,' of His Church.
[2] Phil. ii. 9; cf. Acts iv. 12.   [3] Ps. ii. 7.
[4] 2 Sam. vii. 14; 1 Chron. xxii. 10; Ps. lxxxix. 26, 27.   [5] Heb. ii. 9.

frequently spoke of Himself during His earthly life, since it was as such that He came to redeem mankind, whilst at the same time He constantly refers to His divine origin. The quotations which are chosen from the Old Testament are designed to show that although both angels and men are spoken of as 'sons of God' in the Scriptures the name 'Son' is applied to the Christ, the Messiah, in a unique and singular sense. For no angel is named of God as 'My Son,' nor is it said of any, 'This day have I begotten Thee.'

Here, and in the following verses, we have an example of that spiritual interpretation of the Old Testament Scriptures, of which we have spoken already.[1]

Psalm ii in its literal, historical sense concerns the solemn anointing of David, or some other king, in Zion. Against him are arrayed the hosts of his enemies, but 'the Lord shall have them in derision,' and submit them to the rule of His anointed one. The Jews understood the psalm as applying to the expected Messiah, interpreting it in a spiritual sense, as does the author of Hebrews. The second quotation refers primarily to Solomon, but in a typical, spiritual sense to Christ according to His human nature by which He was descended from David.[2]

And again, when He [that is, God] *bringeth the firstborn into the world He saith, And let all the angels of God worship Him.*

The quotation is from Psalm xcvii. 9 in which God is praised as the King of the whole earth, Who shall come to judgement, and triumph over all evil. Here, what it says of God is applied to Christ, and implies that He is the Son of the God of Whom the psalmist speaks. The words, 'when He bringeth the firstborn into the world,'[3] may well apply both to the Incarnation and to the Second Advent;

---

[1] Cf. p. 13.   [2] Cf. S. Matt. xxii. 41–45; Acts ii. 30–32; Rom. i. 3.
[3] Cf. Heb. x. 5.

but if the psalm is taken in its whole meaning the latter
would seem to be indicated.[1] The phrase, 'when He
bringeth in the firstborn,' or 'first-begotten,' is significant,
for the Greek word translated 'bringeth in' is a legal term
meaning to put one into possession of something, and
Christ is called 'the first-begotten' here, as in Romans
viii. 29, 'the firstborn among many brethren,'[2] as being
the firstborn of all Christians Who has the right of the
inheritance of that kingdom which He has 'opened
to all believers.'[3] So in Colossians i. 18 He is called
'the firstborn from the dead,' as being the first man
to so rise from the grave, whereas in Colossians i. 15,
where He is named 'the firstborn of all creation,' it is
as He Who is 'before all things,' and the Lord and Heir
of all things.

> *And of the angels He saith,*
>> *Who maketh His angels winds,*
>> *And His ministers a flame of fire:*[4]
> *but of the Son He saith,*
>> *Thy throne, O God, is for ever and ever;*
>> *And the sceptre of uprightness is the sceptre of Thy kingdom.*
>> *Thou hast loved righteousness, and hated iniquity;*
>> *Therefore God, Thy God, hath anointed Thee*
>> *With the oil of gladness above Thy fellows.*[5]

The contrast between the Son and the angels is deep-
ened and extended. The angels are servants, who may
be thought of as 'wind and storm fulfilling' God's
word,[6] or as setting in force the powers of nature.[7] But
the Son is an everlasting King, rightly named God
'Whose throne is for ever and ever,' and Who is
anointed, as King, 'with the oil of gladness above' all
created beings.

---

[1] Cf. 1 Cor. xv. 28; Phil. ii. 9, 10; Heb. x. 13.   [2] Cf. Heb. ii. 11, 12.
   [3] *Te Deum.*   [4] Ps. civ. 4.   [5] ibid., xlv. 6, 7.
       [6] ibid., cxlviii. 8.   [7] Cf. S. John v. 4.

And
> *Thou, Lord, in the beginning hast laid the foundation of the earth,*
> *And the heavens are the works of Thy hands;*
> *They shall perish; but Thou continuest:*
> *And they shall all wax old as doth a garment;*
> *And as a mantle shalt Thou wrap them up,*
> *As a garment, and they shall be changed:*
> *But Thou art the same,*
> *And Thy years shall not fail.*[1]

The writer uses the psalm to reassert the truth that it was through Christ, the eternal Son, that the worlds were made, and to compare the changeableness and impermanence of the natural creation with Him Who is 'the Same, yesterday, and to-day, and for ever.'[2]

> *But of which of the angels hath He said at any time,*
> > *Sit Thou on My right hand,*
> > *Till I make Thine enemies the footstool of Thy feet?*[3]
> *Are they not all ministering spirits, sent forth to do service for the sake of them that shall inherit salvation?*

The aptness of the quotation from Psalm cx will be seen when it is remembered that our Lord used these words of Himself.[4] Compared with One so exalted, what are angels but 'ministering spirits' who at His command go forth to do service to men, all of whom are called to inherit salvation?[5]

This belief in the angels as ministering to men is, of course, common to both the Old and New Testaments, and has the support of our Lord Himself, Who can hardly be thought to be making use of an idea derived solely from Persian and Babylonian sources, as some modern critics assert.

---

[1] Ps. cii. 25–27.   [2] Heb. xiii. 8.   [3] Ps. cx. 1.
[4] S. Matt. xxii. 41–45.   [5] Cf. i Tim. ii. 4.

Therefore we ought to give the more earnest heed to the things that were heard, lest haply we drift away from them. For if the word spoken through angels proved steadfast, and every transgression and disobedience received a just recompense of reward; how shall we escape, if we neglect so great salvation? which having at the first been spoken by the Lord, was confirmed unto us by them that heard; God also bearing witness with them, both by signs and wonders, and by manifold powers, and by gifts of the Holy Ghost, according to His will.

'The word spoken through angels' was the Mosaic Law which the Jews believed was given by God, not directly but through angels, and received by the people through Moses. So S. Stephen says of them, 'who have received the Law by the disposition of angels';[1] and S. Paul that 'it was ordained by angels in the hand of a mediator.'[2]

The words 'proved steadfast' mean rested on a sure foundation, and enforced by sanctions, as the following words show. How much greater, then, and worthy of more heed, is the word of salvation first spoken by Jesus, Who is the Word of God in Person, and confirmed by, and communicated to us by, His Apostles,[3] to whom God Himself bare witness by signs and wonders, manifold powers, and gifts of the Holy Ghost.

'Sign' refers to a miracle in its inward character as a means of confirming the truth; 'wonder' to the astonishment which it causes in the beholders; 'power' to its supernatural cause, the power of God. The 'gifts' or 'distributions' of the Holy Ghost are those mentioned by S. Paul, 'diversities of gifts . . . and operations.'[4] 'According to His will' refers to these gifts only, of which S. Paul says, 'He divideth to every man severally as He will.'[5]

---

[1] Acts vii. 53.   [2] Gal. iii. 19.
[3] Cf. Acts ii. 32; iii. 15; 1 S. John i. 1–3, etc.
[4] 1 Cor. xii. 4, 6.   [5] ibid., xii. 11.

COMMENTARY ON THE TEXT: II. 1–8

*For not unto angels did He subject the world to come, whereof
we speak. But one hath somewhere testified, saying:*
    What is man, that Thou art mindful of him?
    Or the son of man, that Thou visitest him?
    Thou madest him a little lower than the angels;
    Thou crownedst him with glory and honour,
    And didst set him over the works of Thy hands:
    Thou hast put all things in subjection under his feet.[1]

'The world to come' is that 'new creation' of the New
Covenant, the 'Church of the firstborn,' of which Christ
is the Head.[2] It is called 'the world to come' here, either
because the writer has in mind its full consummation, for
which we pray, 'Thy kingdom come,' or because he is
thinking of it from the Jewish point of view in which the
history of the world was divided into two ages, that of
'this world or age,' the Old Testament period, and 'the
world or age to come,' the Messianic period. Nowhere
in the Old Testament has God submitted the latter to
angels, but there is a passage, familiar to his readers, in
which 'all things' are said to be subject to man.

The psalm quoted extols the greatness of God as manifested in nature, in comparison with which how in-
significant is man. Yet God has made him but a little
lower than the angels, and crowned him with glory and
honour,[3] and given him dominion over the whole
earth,[4] to which he is far superior, since, as Pascal
says, though the universe crush him, he knows that he is
crushed.

*For in that He subjected all things unto him, He left nothing
that is not subject to him.*

Obviously the writer is speaking of man in his original
state before sin had weakened his sovereignty over nature,
of the consequence of which he goes on to speak.

[1] Ps. viii. 5–7. [2] Cf. Eph. i. 22, 23.
[3] Cf. 'He is the image and glory of God' (1 *Cor.* xi. 7). [4] Gen. i. 26.
D

But now we see not yet all things subjected to him. But we behold Him Who hath been made a little lower than the angels, even Jesus, because of the suffering of death crowned with glory and honour, that by the grace of God He should taste death for every man.

What the psalmist says of man in general is transferred to the Perfect Man, 'the second man, the Lord from heaven,'[1] Who at His Incarnation assumed that human nature which is lower than that of angels by virtue of its being a composite of matter and spirit, and also because great as is the human intellect it is inferior to that of the angels who know directly in an intuitive manner what man only knows from the consideration of external things, and by processes of reasoning.

We behold Jesus, then, during His earthly life, as one Who has become of our race,[2] and shares our infirmities,[3] in order that, by the loving favour of God, He might 'taste of death for every man,' and by so doing merit to be 'crowned with glory and honour,' as S. Paul writes to the Philippians, 'He humbled Himself, becoming obedient unto death, yea, the death of the cross. Wherefore also God highly exalted Him.'[4]

For it became Him [that is, God the Father] *for Whom are all things, and through Whom are all things, in bringing many sons unto glory, to make the Author of their salvation perfect through sufferings. For both He that sanctifieth and they that are sanctified are all of one: for which cause He is not ashamed to call them brethren, saying,*

I will declare thy name unto My brethren.

In the midst of the congregation will I sing thy praise.[5]

And again, I will put My trust in Him. And again, Behold I, and the children which God hath given Me.[6]

'For it became Him.' This must not be understood as implying any necessity on the part of God Himself, since He is entirely free, and unconstrained by anything outside

---

[1] 1 Cor. xv. 47; cf. Eph. i. 22.   [2] Cf. Heb. v. 14
[3] ibid., iv. 15.   [4] Phil. ii. 8, 9.
[5] Ps. xxii. 22.   [6] Isa. viii. 17, 18 (Septuagint).

Himself. But if we look at the means which God, by a free
act of His love, took to redeem mankind, we may see how
fitting, in view of man's nature and fallen condition, they
were. It became Him in somewhat of the way in which it
becomes a man to act according to his nature.

'For Whom . . . through Whom . . .' God is the final
cause (the end for which anything is made or done), for
Whom all things were created, and the efficient cause (the
agent by whom something is done) of all things.

The rest of this passage must be read as a whole. The
meaning is: God willed to restore man to that sonship
which he had forfeited by his sin, and which he could
not recover by himself. Yet, since the sin was his, it was
fitting that he should 'work out his own salvation,[1] which
was only possible through suffering. God, therefore, sent
His Son, 'in the likeness of sinful flesh,'[2] to suffer on man's
behalf (not in place of man), that He might become the
Author or Leader of their salvation, Who first takes part
in what, by His aid and example, man must do. The
Greek word 'to perfect' means, to bring to an end or goal,
to cause some one or something to be perfected, and as
applied here to our Lord can only refer to His human
nature, and to His life on earth during which, as Man, He
experienced the conditions and sufferings of men, and as
Man was crowned with the glory and honour of His
Resurrection and session at the right hand of His Father,
human nature in Him, its Head and Representative, thus
attaining its final and perfecting goal.[3] 'For both He that
sanctifieth . . . are all of one' origin and race, descended
from one common father, Adam, according to the flesh.
This, in view of what follows, 'For this cause, He is not
ashamed to call them brethren,' seems to be the meaning,
but some commentators prefer to make 'of one' refer to
God, the Creator of all men. If this interpretation be

[1] Phil. ii. 13.   [2] Rom. viii. 3; cf. Heb. ii. 17.
[3] The question of how Christ can be said to be perfected will be dealt
with in the commentary on chapter v. 8, 9.

adopted, a distinction must be made between the unique
Sonship of Christ and that common to all men, whilst
at the same time the statement 'He is not ashamed' may
be taken to imply 'in spite of their fallen condition.'

*Since, then, the children are sharers in flesh and blood, He also
Himself partook of the same; that through death He might bring
to nought him that had the power of death, that is, the devil; and
might deliver all them who through fear of death were all their
lifetime subject to bondage.*

Here, as all through his Epistle, the writer states clearly
the object for which God became man. It was not, as is
too commonly thought to-day, simply to be a Teacher
and Example, but to be our Redeemer and Saviour. The
whole tenor of the New Testament shows that it is not the
moral teaching (for example, of the Sermon on the
Mount) or our Lord's acts of kindness which are central,
but His Death and Resurrection. The Gospels, especially
S. Mark, which contains our Lord's own words, 'The Son
of man came . . . to give His life a ransom for many,' are
concerned with showing how Jesus came to His Passion,
the account of which occupies more space, and is given in
greater detail, than anything else. The apostolic preaching is entirely devoted to it.[1] The Epistles emphasize it
on almost every page. To dilute this universal witness of
the first Christians, to reduce the Passion of the Lord to
no more than the death of a great teacher, as is the
Modernist mood, is to deprive the New Testament of any
claim to serious consideration and to rob Christianity of the
one thing which both makes it unique among all the great
religions of the world, and justifies its claim to be necessary
for all men and all time. The devil is said to have 'the power
of death' inasmuch as he is the author of sin, the consequence of which is both spiritual and physical death.[2]

[1] Cf. Acts ii and following chapters.
[2] Gen. iii. 3; Rom. v. 12; vi. 16, 21, 23; S. Jas. i. 15, etc.; Wisd. ii. 24,
'Through envy of the devil came death into the world.'

Many such passages clearly refer to physical death, which has not been abolished, nor do the above words claim that it has, only that he who had the power of death has been vanquished, and mankind delivered from the fear of death. For, made 'partakers of Christ,' we 'are saved by His life,'[1] which, communicated to us in Baptism,[2] avails for our whole body-soul nature, as our Lord Himself teaches.[3]

In verse 10 the writer had spoken of Christ as tasting death for every man, and this recalls our Lord's words, as repeated by the Jews, 'If a man keep My saying, he shall never taste of death.'[4] Archbishop W. Temple translates 'he shall not notice death,' and comments that our Lord is not promising 'that any one who keeps His word shall avoid the physical incident called death; but that if his mind is turned toward that word it will not pay attention to death . . . it happens to him, but he does not in any full sense see or notice it.'[5]

'The sting of death is sin,'[6] of which death is the consequence, and which causes the fear spoken of. There is also the fear caused both by the fact that death is an unnatural thing, 'for God made not death,' but 'created man to be immortal;'[7] and, before Christ came, the dread of that unknown 'bourne from which no traveller had returned.' The latter is seen in the prayer of Hezekiah,[8] and in the last reported words of Aristotle, 'Naked came I into this world, in misery have I lived, in doubt I die; I know not what shall become of me; do Thou, Being of all beings, have mercy on me.'

From this bondage to sin and fear we have been delivered by our Lord, 'Thanks be to God Who giveth us the victory through our Lord Jesus Christ.'[9]

[1] Rom. v. 10.
[2] ibid., vi. 4, 5; Gal. iii. 27; Col. ii. 12; Titus iii. 5, etc.
[3] S. John vi. 51, 54.   [4] ibid., viii. 52.
[5] *Readings in S. John's Gospel*, vol. i, pp. 146–7.   [6] 1 Cor. xv. 56.
[7] Wisd. i. 13; ii. 23.   [8] Isa. xxxviii. 18.   [9] 1 Cor. xv. 54–57.

*For verily not of angels doth He take hold, but He taketh hold
of the seed of Abraham. Wherefore it behoved Him in all things
to be made like unto His brethren, that He might be a merciful
and faithful high priest in things pertaining to God, to make
propitiation for the sins of the people. For in that He Himself hath
suffered being tempted, He is able to succour them that are tempted.*

'For verily not of angels,' the 'for verily' means, 'for
as we well know,' and 'take hold,' in the Greek, 'in order
to help.' The verse gives the reason for the Incarnation
in which God became man in order to redeem man, not
angels.

'Of the seed,' that is, of the race and faith of Abraham
to whom the promise 'in thee shall all families of the earth
be blessed,' was made.[1]

'It behoved Him . . .' It was fitting that the High
Priest of humanity should share in our nature, so that
uniting it to His divine nature[2] He might renew it 'after
the image' according to which it was created.[3] Moreover,
in order to reconcile man to God, He must do, as man,
that which man had refused to do, that is, offer to God
the sacrifice which represented the worship, obedience,
and love which was due to Him. His divinely appointed
office was that of the one Mediator between God and
man. 'There is one Mediator between God and men,
Himself man, Christ Jesus, Who gave Himself a ransom
for all.'[4] To be such a mediator He must be faithful 'in all
things pertaining to God,' of which things worship is the
first, and merciful towards men. For the latter He added
to the mercy of God as God, His human experience of
man's infirmity, inasmuch as He suffered temptation,[5]
so gaining a human sympathy and compassion for men
which enables Him 'to succour them that are tempted,'
and gives them 'boldness' to draw near unto the throne
of grace for mercy and 'grace to help in time of need.'[6]

---

[1] Gen. xii. 2, 3; S. Luke i. 55; Gal. iii. 7–14, etc.
[2] Cf. 2 S. Pet. i. 4.   [3] Col. iii. 10.
[4] 1 Tim. ii. 5.   [5] Cf. S. Luke iv. 2; x. 25.   [6] Heb. iv. 15, 16.

Wherefore, holy brethren, partakers of a heavenly calling, con-sider the Apostle and High Priest of our confession, even Jesus.

'Wherefore,' that is, because He is a merciful and faith-ful High Priest, consider, give attention to Jesus, the Apostle Whom God has sent to proclaim His will to men.[1]

'Holy brethren, partakers . . .' Holy, both in the Old Testament sense of the word, 'chosen' for a particular mission, as were the Jewish people, and in the developed New Testament sense, made holy by their union with Christ, 'that we might be partakers of His holiness,'[2] 'perfecting holiness in the fear of the Lord.'[3]

'Our confession' of the Faith revealed in and by Jesus, *Who was faithful to Him Who appointed Him, as also was Moses in all His house. For He [Jesus] hath been counted as worthy of more glory than Moses, by so much as He that built the house hath more honour than the house. For every house is builded by some one; but He that built all things is God. And Moses, indeed, was faithful in all His house as a servant, for a testimony of those things which were afterward to be spoken; but Christ, as a Son, over His house; Whose house we are, if we hold fast our boldness and the glorying of our hope firm unto the end.*

Having shown that, as the Son of God, Christ is uniquely superior to the angels, through whom the ancient Law was ministered, the writer goes on to show His superiority to Moses, through whom that Law was transmittted to the people. Moses, indeed, was a faithful servant in God's House, as Israel was always called.[4] But Jesus is worthy of much higher honour, as he that builds a house has more honour than the house, and He that built and established this House is God, Who built all things. Emphasis is given to this by the fact that the Greek word means, not simply to build, but also to furnish and arrange

[1] Cf. S. John v. 37, 43; vi. 38; vii. 16; xvii. 3, 7, 8, 18; xx. 21; Gal. iv. 4, etc.
[2] Heb. xii. 10.   [3] 2 Cor. vii. 1.
[4] Num. xx. 29; Ps. xcviii. 3; Isa. v. 7; Acts ii. 36, etc.

everything in the house, including the staff. Moses, then, was a servant *in* God's House, but Jesus is Son *over* His own House, 'Whose House we are,' the 'household of God.'[1]

'If we hold fast . . . unto the end.' They had begun well, and persevered for a time,[2] but were now in danger of loosening their hold on the Faith and of falling away. But the Christian Faith and life is all concerned with, and directed to an end, a fulfilment, a perfecting, which end is none other than God Himself, to Whom Christ is the Way. The Greek word translated 'boldness' means freedom or boldness of speech, and so, confidence,[3] in which they are to glory and stretch forward to the hope which is set before them.[4]

> *Wherefore, as the Holy Ghost saith,*
> *To-day if ye shall hear His voice,*
> *Harden not your hearts, as in the provocation,*
> *Like as in the day of temptation in the wilderness,*
> *Wherewith your fathers tempted Me by proving Me,*
> *And saw My works forty years.*
> *Wherefore I was displeased with this generation,*
> *And said, They do alway err in their heart:*
> *As I sware in My wrath,*
> *They shall not enter into My rest.*[5]

The section iii. 7–iv. 13, is devoted to a solemn warning, reinforced by the past history of their race, against the sins of unbelief, and disobedience to the word of God.

'As the Holy Ghost saith.' 'God is the primary Author of Holy Scripture, the actual writers are instruments inspired by Him.'[6] Both the Old and New Testaments contain the record of God's revelation of Himself and His will, and of the two Covenants, the first made to His chosen

---

[1] Eph. ii. 19.   [2] Cf. Heb. vi. 9, 10; x. 32–35.
[3] Cf. ibid., iii. 6.   [4] Cf. ibid., vi. 17–20.   [5] Ps. xcv.
[6] Vide p. 15; cf. Rom. ix. 22–26; 2 Cor. vi. 1, 2, 17; Eph. iv. 8; Heb. i. 5–13; v. 5, 6; viii. 8–12; x. 15; 2 S. Pet. i. 21.

people, Israel, the second to the Church. Thus S. Paul, referring to the Old Testament Scriptures, writes to Timothy, 'from a babe thou hast known the sacred writings which are able to make thee wise unto salvation through faith in Christ Jesus. Every Scripture inspired of God is also profitable for teaching, for reproof, for correction, for instruction in righteousness.'[1]

'To-day,' this present day no less than that day long past,[2] is God's to-day. 'For Thou art most high, and art not changed, neither in Thee doth to-day ever pass away. . . . How many of our fathers' years have already passed away through Thy To-day, and from it received the measure and mould of their being such as it was. But Thou art still the same and all things of to-morrow, and all beyond it, and all of yesterday, and all behind it, Thou hast done in this Thy to-day.'[3]

'As in the provocation . . .' This refers to the event recorded in Exodus xvii, Numbers xx, and Deuteronomy xxxiii. 8, in which the Israelites murmured against Moses, whose prayer God answered by giving them water out of the rock, and named the place, Massah, that is, temptation, and Meribah, that is, contention. There, the Israelites had failed in faith, saying, 'Is the Lord among us or not?' They 'proved' God, that is, desired a visible proof of His presence which He gave them, as He did repeatedly during the forty years in the wilderness. 'They tempted Me, and tested Me; yet they saw My work,' in spite of which they failed to recognize His proving or testing of them.[4] So 'I was displeased' (the Hebrew text reads, 'I loathed, was weary of them'), for 'they do alway err in their hearts,' or as the Septuagint version reads, 'they have not known My ways,' that is, here, the way in which God wills them to walk. In other passages it sometimes means, God's own ways, as

---

[1] 2 Tim. iii. 15, 16; cf. 1 Cor. x. 1–11; S. Luke xxiv. 44–47, etc.
[2] Cf. 2 Cor. vi. 2.   [3] S. Augustine, *Confessions*, i. 6.
[4] Cf. Deut. viii. 2, 3.

in Psalm xxv. 10, 'All the ways of the Lord are mercy and truth,' and 'Neither are your ways My ways.'[1]

'My rest.' The rest primarily referred to is the possession of the land which God had promised to Abraham,[2] the peaceful possession of which depended upon Israel's obedience to God.[3] This they failed to render so that the evils spoken of in verses 15–end fell upon them, and in their later history a more spiritual conception of the promised land began to be held by many, though this, again, was obscured by the nationalistic outlook which finally brought about the destruction of Jerusalem, and the scattering of the Jews throughout the world. To the Christians the promised rest of Canaan was but a type, and foreshadowing, of the true rest in God which Christ has promised to those who hope in Him.

Take heed, brethren, lest haply there shall be in any one of you an evil heart of unbelief, in falling away from the living God: but exhort one another day by day, so long as it is called To-day; lest any one of you be hardened by the deceitfulness of sin: for we are become partakers of Christ, if we hold fast the beginning of our confidence unto the end: while it is said,

To-day if ye shall hear His voice,
Harden not your hearts, as in the provocation.

'An evil heart of unbelief,' that is, a heart inclined to unbelief through its perverseness, which may easily lead to a falling away from Him Who is, as He has ever been, the' living God.'

'So long as it is called To-day,' the To-day in which God calls more clearly than of old, the To-day of which our Lord speaks, 'We must work the works of Him that sent Me, while it is day: the night cometh when no man can work.'[4]

'Hardened by the deceitfulness of sin,' alluring with

[1] Isa. lv. 8, 9.　　[2] Gen. xii. 7; xvii. 8.
[3] Deut. xxviii.　　[4] S. John ix. 4; cf. xi. 9, 10.

fair promises and specious arguments which, if listened to, result in a hardening of the heart, and a moral and spiritual insensitiveness to truth and grace such as the Apostle describes, 'They became vain in their reasonings, and their senseless heart was darkened,'[1] 'alienated from the life of God because of the ignorance that is in them, because of the hardening of their heart.'[2]

'We are become . . . if we hold fast . . .' The Greek of the second half of this sentence reads, 'If we hold fast the beginning of his substance unto the end.' The word 'substance' has three meanings: foundation, confidence, and the essence, the substantial being, of a thing. It should be read here in relation to, 'We are become partakers of Christ,' and thus means, We have been united to Christ, made one with Him, members of His Body, the Church,[3] in Baptism, which we received by faith, which thus is the beginning or principle of our Christian being and life.[4] This gives us a strong confidence which must be held fast unto the end. For as S. Jerome says, 'In Christians it is not the beginning but the end which is required.'[5] The truth is that we are made Christians by an act of God, but we become, grow up to be good Christians, by our own efforts, inspired and aided by grace. What we have received as a free gift must not only be held fast, but also used, increased, developed unto perfection.

For who, when they heard, did provoke? nay, did not all they that came out of Egypt by Moses? And with whom was He displeased forty years? was it not with them that sinned, whose carcases fell in the wilderness? And to whom sware He that they should not enter into His rest, but to them that were disobedient? And we see that they were not able to enter in because of unbelief.

[1] Rom. i. 21.   [2] Eph. iv. 18.
[3] Cf. S. John xv. 1-4; 1 Cor. xii. 12; 2 S. Pet. i. 4.
[4] Cf. Gal. ii. 20.   [5] Cf. S. Matt. xxiv. 13; Phil. iii. 12-14.

The point of this passge is, that the people who came out of Egypt, with whom God was displeased, who perished in the wilderness, were those for whom God had done great things, such as merited their faith and trust in Him. It was precisely the lack of such faith which led them to murmuring, impatience, and disobedience. So would the writer emphasize the sinful character of unbelief, especially in those who had had so many signs of God's favour toward them.

Let us fear therefore, lest haply, a promise being left of entering His rest, any one of you should seem to come short of it. For indeed we have had good tidings preached to us, even as also they: but the word of hearing did not profit them because they were not united by faith with them that heard.

What befell them may befall us who have had even better tidings, the good news of the Gospel, preached to us. Let us take heed lest by unbelief we fall short, fail to attain to the fullness of the promises of Christ.

The rest of the passage, in the original, is capable o more than one interpretation. The one given above implies that the hearing of God's word did not profit the people of Israel in general because they had not the faith which possessed Moses and Joshua. A more likely meaning is that although they heard with their ears the word of God communicated to them through Moses, they lacked the inward faith which would receive it, and cause it to bear fruit in their lives. They were of those of whom our Lord speaks, 'Seeing they see not, and hearing they hear not, neither do they understand.'[1] Of the meaning and effects of faith we shall read later on. Here the emphasis is on its power to receive and assimilate inwardly what we hear outwardly of the word of God.

For we which have believed do enter into that rest; even as He hath said,

As I sware in My wrath,

[1] S. Matt. xiii. 13; cf. Rom. xi. 20–22.

They shall not enter into My rest,
although the works were finished from the foundation of the
world.

'We do enter,' that is, we are already entering into that rest of God by faith, being made inheritors of the kingdom of God.[1] The repetition of the words 'As I sware . . .' is meant to emphasize the fact that the true rest of God still remains, though they to whom it was first promised failed to enter owing to their unbelief. 'My rest' is here taken in a spiritual sense of God's abiding rest, for His work was finished when the world was created.

For He hath said somewhere of the seventh day on this wise,
And God rested on the seventh day from all His works;[2] and in
this place again,
They shall not enter into My rest.

The attribution of the words of Genesis to God Himself as the primary Author of Scripture should be noted. Also the statement that God's work was 'finished,' upon which He 'rested,' must not be understood in the sense we might use those terms of ourselves, as, for instance, when we say, 'I have finished my work and shall sit down and rest.' Here, the writer is referring only to the work of Creation which was finished in a certain period of time (which Genesis speaks of as 'days' without intending to suggest days of twenty-four hours each, but only the order in which things were created), and finished in the sense that all that was necessary for their being and development had been given them. God, then, rested from the work He had so far done in bringing about the genesis, the beginning of the physical universe, but not in the sense of 'sitting back and doing nothing,' while the universe continued to exist 'on its own.' For He is not only the Creator but also the Sustainer of all things, whose ever-creative act keeps all things in their being. Thus our

[1] Cf. Heb. xii. 22–24; Rom. iii. 22, 23.   [2] Gen. ii. 2, 3.

Lord says, 'My Father worketh hitherto, and I work,'[1]
and 'I have finished [that is, accomplished, consummated]
the work which Thou gavest Me to do,'[2] meaning that all
had been done for the redemption and salvation of men,
since all that was still to be done by the preaching of the
Gospel and the ministering of grace was summed up in,
and owed all to, His consummation of the Father's will.

The rest of God, into which we are called to enter, is
not an idle passivity, the doing of 'nothing for ever and
ever,' but the highest activity, without anything of that
fatigue, or monotony, or change, or lack of full satisfaction
which our present activity entails. Here we need change,
the alternation of activity and rest, one aiding the other;
there both are one in that sight of God as He is which,
possessed and enjoyed, can never be completely comprehended, nor ever cease to be our fullest satisfaction and
unending delight.

*Seeing therefore it remaineth that some should enter thereinto,
and they to whom the good tidings were before preached failed
to enter in because of disobedience, He again defineth a certain
day, saying in David, after so long a time, To-day, as it hath
been before said,*
　　To-day if ye shall hear His voice,
　　Harden not your hearts.
*For if Joshua had given them rest, He would not have spoken
afterward of another day. There remaineth therefore a sabbath
rest for the people of God. For he that is entered into his rest
hath himself also rested from all his works, as God did from
His.*

The good tidings of that 'To-day' of old had not pene-
trated into the hearts of those to whom it was addressed,
yet God's To-day is not limited by time, nor His promise
made void by their disobedience. 'After so long a time'
since that failure of faith, the psalmist calls to those of his

---

[1] S. John v. 17.　　　[2] ibid., xvii. 4.

own time for an act of faith in God, 'O come, let us worship and bow down: let us kneel before the Lord our
Maker, for He is *our* God,' and now is His To-day.
'Harden not your hearts,' as did your fathers in the day
of trial in the wilderness. And what was true in David's
day is even more true in this To-day in which God has
spoken by His Son of that eternal rest which remaineth
for His people, a rest which is as the rest of God Himself.

Let us therefore give diligence to enter into that rest, that no
man fall after the same example of disobedience. For the word
of God is living and active, and sharper than any two-edged sword,
and piercing even to the dividing of soul and spirit, of both joints
and marrow, and quick to discern the thoughts and intents of the
heart. And there is no creature that is not manifest in His sight:
but all things are naked and laid open before the eyes of Him
with Whom we have to do.

The 'word of God' is primarily God's word to man,
but also 'The Word' of Whom S. John speaks,[1] the Son
of God. The context shows that the writer is thinking of
the word of promise spoken of old, and insisting that it is
still 'living and active, and sharper than any two-edged
sword,'[2] for it pierces to and divides the innermost soul
and spirit. Soul and spirit are not two different things,
but the one human soul which fulfils two different functions. By the soul is meant the spiritual principle in man
which animates the body, enabling it to act as a body.
By the spirit is meant the higher spiritual activities of
the soul, those of the mind and will, by which man is
capable of coming into communion with God Who is
Spirit. So does the word of God pierce man's spiritual
nature as a sword of steel pierces and divides his body.
Even more so, for it reaches to his very thoughts and
intentions whilst they are still hidden in the heart. For
we have to reckon with a God Who knows all things, even
those which we try to hide from ourselves.

[1] S. John i. 1, 14; Rev. xix. 13.   [2] Cf. Rev. i. 16.

Having then a great High Priest, Who hath passed through the heavens, Jesus the Son of God, let us hold fast our profession. For we have not a High Priest that cannot be touched with the feeling of our infirmities; but one that hath been in all points tempted like as we are, yet without sin. Let us therefore draw near with boldness unto the throne of grace, that we may receive mercy, and may find grace to help in time of need.

Before passing to the elucidation of the High Priesthood of Christ, the writer reiterates the main truths about the Personality of our Lord. He is the Son of God in the literal and unique sense of the word, the true, eternal image of the being, nature, and life of God, 'of one substance with the Father,' by Whom all things were created, and are upheld in being and existence. No less is He of one being, nature, and life with man, having by His Incarnation taken the fullness of our humanity of a human mother.[1] Thus He is the true and sole Mediator between God and man, He Who reveals God to man more fully than could the prophets of old, and represents and presents man to God as the High Priest of humanity Who, having made 'purification for sins,' by tasting 'death for every man,' has entered into the rest of God, and is for ever crowned with glory and honour' at His right hand.

This is the truth which we have received from the apostolic witnesses, and which we must cling to, for in it lies our salvation. Our faith must not waver, lest we fall away into that unbelief and disobedience by which Israel forfeited the promise of God. We indeed have a greater incentive to faith in that the Captain of our salvation has shared in our infirmities and trials, and thus has a truly human knowledge of them, and the deepest sympathy with us. He not only knows them as God, but as Man Who has actually experienced them, knows after our manner what it is to be tired,[2] hungry, thirsty,[3] dis-

---

[1] Cf. Gal. iv. 4; Col. ii. 9, etc.   [2] S. John iv. 6.

[3] ibid., xix. 28.

appointed,[1] tempted,[2] mocked,[3] persecuted,[4] to suffer in
body and mind,[5] and to endure the worst of deaths. And
all this was intensified in Him, not only by the perfection
of His human nature which made Him more sensitive
than those whose nature has been coarsened by sin, but
also because He never yielded to temptation, and so
experienced its power to the uttermost, as none do who
at some point give way.

Such is He Who, in our nature, having endured and
conquered, 'has passed through the heavens,' as the
Apostles saw Him ascend until 'a cloud received Him
out of their sight,'[6] to the glory of God, the Blessed
Trinity. This is the source and foundation of our confidence, in which we ought to draw near boldly to the
throne of grace, that we may 'receive' mercy, God's free
gift to the undeserving, and by desire and prayer 'find'
the grace to help in time of need. For it is in such
times, not when we are praying, that God answers our
cry for His help.

*For every high priest, being taken from among men, is appointed
for men in things pertaining to God, that he may offer both gifts
and sacrifices for sins: who can bear gently with the ignorant and
erring, for that he himself is compassed with infirmity; and by
reason thereof is bound, as for the people, so also for himself, to
offer for sins. And no man taketh this honour unto himself, but
when he is called of God, even as was Aaron.*

In these words we have a summary of the character
and office of priesthood. A priest is a man who is set
apart from his fellows by a definite and authoritative
appointment in order that he may act for men in the
things which concern man's relation to God, the chief
of which are the offering of gifts and sacrifices for sins.
Being a man who must offer such sacrifices for his own

---

[1] S. Mark vi. 6.   [2] S. Matt. iv. 1; xxii. 18, etc.
[3] S. Luke xvi. 14; xxiii. 11.   [4] S. Matt. xii. 14, etc.
[5] ibid., xxvi. 37; xxvii. 27.   [6] Acts i. 9.

E

sins, as for others, he is eminently fitted 'to bear gently
with the ignorant and erring,' since he himself is of their
number. No man may appoint himself to an office of
such dignity; he must have been 'called of God even as
was Aaron.'[1]

The accounts of the call of Aaron and the Levites to
the priesthood make it clear that the call was not an
inward one such as might determine a man to seek the
priesthood, but an outward one, a command given by
God through Moses. Nor was it based on moral qualifica-
tions, but simply on the will and choice of God Himself.
In like manner did our Lord choose and appoint His
priests.[2]

A priest is a mediator who stands between man and
God, not to prevent or hinder man's approach to God,
but to minister the means by which he is united to God.
He is as a bridge, not a gulf, and is so constituted by God
Who alone can bridge the gulf between Himself and man,
one both of nature and of sin.

Now Christ was, and is, such a High Priest, for—
So Christ also glorified not Himself to be made a high priest, but
  He that spake unto Him,
    Thou art My Son,
    This day have I begotten Thee:
as He saith also in another place,
    Thou art a priest for ever
    After the order of Melchizedek.
Who in the days of His flesh, having offered up prayers and
supplications with strong crying and tears unto Him that was
able to save Him from death, and having been heard for His
godly fear though He was a Son, yet learned obedience by the
things which He suffered; and having been made perfect, He
became unto all that obey Him the Author of eternal salvation;
named of God a high priest after the order of Melchizedek.

[1] Exod. xxviii. 1; xl. 12–15; Lev. viii. 1–13; Num. iii. 1–10; xviii. 1–7.
[2] S. Matt. x. 1; S. John xv. 16; xx. 21; S. Luke vi. 16.

What was true of the Jewish high priest is now shown to be true of Christ, Who did not take upon Himself the dignity and office of High Priesthood, but received it from the Father. The first quotation refers to the Resurrection,[1] wherein the Father witnessed to the divine Sonship of Jesus,[2] and glorified Him as the Sovereign Ruler over all things.[3] The second declares that He was also given an eternal Priesthood according to the order and manner of that of Melchizedek. What were the distinctive characteristics of that order will be seen in chapter vii.

But our Lord also fulfils the second condition of priesthood, that of having a personal, human experience of man's infirmity and temptations. For 'in the days of His flesh,' that is, of His life on earth when being Man He could 'feel'[4] our weakness and trials both mentally and physically, in a way which God, being Spirit, does not, 'offered up prayers and supplications' unto His Father Who had the power to 'save Him from death.' The reference is to our Lord's agony in the Garden, wherein He prayed, 'Father, all things are possible unto Thee; remove this cup [of torture and death] from Me: howbeit not what I will, but what Thou wilt,'[5] and was heard because of His reverence and willing obedience to the Father's will. But, it may be asked, how can it be said that He was heard? The answer is that He made His prayer to be saved from death entirely conditional on the will of His Father, 'Not what I will, but what Thou wilt.' What was heard, and answered, was His willing acceptance of that will, whatever it might be. His human nature shrank from the Passion, His human will had no desire but to fulfil the divine will.[6]

'He learned' by practical experience of suffering, the virtue of obedience, 'and having been perfected.' But how could Christ, being God, and so possessing all know-

[1] Cf. Acts xiii. 32, 33.
[2] Cf. Heb. i. 4, 5; S. John xvii. 1, 2; Rom. i. 1–4.
[3] Eph. i. 20–23.
[4] Heb. iv. 15.
[5] S. Mark xiv. 36.
[6] Cf. S. John vi. 38.

ledge, 'in Whom are all the treasures of wisdom and knowledge,'[1] learn, that is, acquire knowledge? Did not He Who was the eternal Word possess all knowledge? Yes, nor did He lay aside His divine knowledge which He shared with the Father when He became Man. But in so doing, in entering human-wise into our human conditions and experience He gained a human knowledge in a human way. And though this is part of that mystery of the union of two natures in the one Person of Christ which is beyond our full comprehension, it may be illustrated by the fact that any one of us may gain a knowledge of a particular subject in more than one way. A knowledge of Italian art, or of a foreign country, may be gained by reading about and seeing pictures of it; or by studying the originals in the churches and galleries of Europe; or, in the case of a country, by living in it. And such knowledge may be greatly increased in the first case by studying and practising the technique of painting. Each of these methods is different, though relating to the same subject, and each extends one's knowledge by adding a new, experimental point of view to those already acquired. The illustration must not be pressed too closely, since it does not adequately explain the manner in which our Lord grew in knowledge.

The Greek word here translated 'perfected' means, to bring some one or something to an end, a goal, and so to consummate and perfect. Thus our Lord, having reached the appointed goal of His earthly life, says, 'I have consummated the work Thou gavest Me to do,'[1] and again, on the Cross, 'It is consummated.'[2] 'Having been made perfect,' then, has the same meaning as in chapter ii. 11, that is, that as Man He had reached the divinely ordained end of His life on earth, the fact being attested by His Resurrection by which He entered, in our human nature, into the glory for which He had prayed, 'And now, O Father, glorify Thou Me with Thine own self

[1] Col. ii. 3.   [2] S. John xvii. 4.   [3] ibid., xix. 30.

with the glory which I had with Thee before the world
was.'[1] And since all this was done in our nature, and as
the Head and Representative of the whole human race,
He thus 'became the Author of eternal salvation unto all
them that obey Him,' for obedience is the proof of our
faith in, and our love for, Him.[2]

Of whom we have many things to say, and hard of interpretation,
seeing ye are become dull of hearing. For when by reason of the
time [since you became Christians] *ye ought to be teachers, you*
have need again that some one teach you the rudiments of the first
principles of the oracles of God; and are become such as have need
of milk, and not of solid food. For every one that partaketh of
milk is without experience of the word of righteousness, for [as
regards this] *he is a babe. But solid food is for full-grown men,*
even those who by reason of use have their [spiritual] *senses*
exercised to discern good and evil.

The temptation to apostasize from the Faith is not
altogether, or even chiefly, due to external persecution.
This they had endured after their conversion when they
became a 'laughing-stock' to their Jewish neighbours, and
'took joyfully' the loss of their possessions.[3] But now the
real danger lay within, was of an interior, spiritual
character, the consequence of the fact that they had
become 'dull of hearing,' that is, of a mental and spiritual
apprehension and receptivity of the meaning and implications of the Christian Faith. They had been content to
remain as babes in the kindergarten instead of growing
up in the knowledge and appreciation of the truths of the
Gospel, and it was this which now weakened their re-
sistance to the exterior pressure of persecution. It is
this condition of spiritual infancy which makes what he
has to say about Christ hard for them to understand, for
it is the solid food of full-grown men compared to the
milk which is all that babes may assimilate. To be capable

---

[1] ibid., xvii. 5.   [2] ibid., xiv. 23, 24.   [3] Heb. x. 32–34.

of profiting by such food they ought to have exercised
their spiritual senses so as to have become able to distin-
guish between good and evil, the true and the false.

*Wherefore let us cease to speak of the first principles of Christ,
and press on to perfection; not laying again a foundation of repentance from dead works, and of faith towards God, of the teaching
of baptisms, and of laying on of hands, and of resurrection of the
dead, and of eternal judgement. And this we will do if God
permit.*

The foundation of the first principles of Christian Faith
has been laid, and although they have failed to build
themselves upon it, he will not go over it again, since
what they need now is to pass from merely leaning on
what they know to an active pressing on to the perfection
of which those principles are but the preliminary steps.
What they need is to see whither those first steps were
designed to lead them.

The principles mentioned are those upon which the
apostolic preaching was based.[1] Repentance, change of
mind, was the first word of the preaching of our Lord
as it had been of the Baptist.[2] 'Dead works' are those
which done apart from Christ have no value as regards
the true purpose of human life, 'Without Me ye can do
nothing.'[3] The writer may be referring more particularly
to the works of the Old Covenant, as he does later, 'How
much more shall the blood of Christ . . . cleanse your
conscience from dead works to serve the living God?'[4]
The wider application of the word to all sin may be
noted.[5]

'Faith towards God' means more than believing in His
existence; it implies the movement of the will in desire,
and so of some love for God. 'The teaching of baptisms,'

---

[1] Cf. Acts ii. 38; iv. 2, 33; viii. 14–17, etc.
[2] S. Mark i. 4, 14, 15.   [3] S. John xv. 5; cf. Rom. xi. 6.
[4] Heb. ix. 14; cf. Gal. ii. 16; iii. 2, 10.
[5] Rom. xiii. 12; Gal. v. 19; Eph. v. 11.

that is, about baptisms, the word being in the plural because Christian teaching would emphasize the difference between Jewish ablutions such as were common under the Law,[1] and that given by S. John the Baptist and Christian Baptism.[2]

'Laying on of hands,' common amongst the Jews as a sign of blessing, or consecration to some office,[3] was used also by our Lord[4] and by the Apostles,[5] especially in conferring Confirmation and Ordination, as an outward sign of the particular grace given in these Sacraments.

The doctrines of the resurrection from the dead and of eternal judgement form an essential part of our Lord's teaching, and so of His Church.[6]

Of these fundamental truths he will not stop to speak, partly because they know them, however imperfectly, and will understand them better in the light of what he is about to say. But there is also another reason, of deeper import.

For as touching those who were once enlightened and tasted of the heavenly gift, and were made partakers of the Holy Ghost, and tasted the good word of God, and the powers of the age to come, and then fell away, it is impossible to renew them again unto repentance; seeing they crucify to themselves the Son of God afresh, and put Him to an open shame. For the land which hath drunk the rain that cometh oft upon it, and bringeth forth herbs meet for them for whose sake it is also tilled, receiveth blessing from God: but if it beareth thorns and thistles, it is rejected, and nigh unto a curse; whose end is to be burned.

Let us paraphrase: 'For concerning those who were instructed in the Christian Faith, and illuminated in

---

[1] Cf. Exod. xxix. 4; Lev. xiv. 8, 9; 2 Chron. iv. 6.
[2] Cf. Acts xix. 1–6.   [3] Gen. xlviii. 13; Num. xxvii. 18; Lev. iii. 2.
[4] S. Luke iv. 40, etc.   [5] Acts vi. 6; viii. 17; xix. 6; 1 Tim. v. 22.
[6] S. Mark x. 33, 34; xii. 26, 27; 1 Cor. xv. 4, 12–22, etc.; S. Matt. xxv. 31–46; S. John v. 22, 24, 27; 2 Tim. iv. 1, etc.

Baptism by Christ, the true Light, and experienced the heavenly gift of eternal life in Him, and received the Holy Ghost in Confirmation, and already have by faith experienced the good promises of God, and the power of His grace actively present in His Church, and after all this have renounced the Faith, it is humanly impossible, by reiterating the truths they were taught and believed for a time, to bring them to repentance. For by their apostasy they have taken part with those who crucified Christ, and so put Him to shame before men. They have become like a piece of waste land, good for nothing, bearing only thorns and thistles.'

'Enlightened,' both by the teaching given before Baptism and by Baptism itself. The latter was often called the Sacrament of illumination.

'Tasted,' were conscious of the new life, received in Baptism, and of the truth and grace by which it was nourished.

'It is impossible' for men to bring them to repentance, not impossible to God. Experience in dealing with people who have forsaken the Faith for some other religion shows how true this is.

'Crucify to themselves the Son of God afresh.' Not that Christ can be crucified, or suffer in any way in Himself. To the meaning given in the above paraphrase a further one is suggested by the words 'to themselves.' As our Lord and the Apostles teach, Christ dwells in the Christian soul.[1] But sin of the quality of apostasy severs that union, the indwelling Christ is crucified within the soul which suffers the loss of the Saviour it has denied. 'For if we sin wilfully after that we have received the knowledge of the truth there remaineth no more a sacrifice for sins.'[2] It should be noted that both passages refer to those who have accepted 'the truth as it is in Jesus,'[3] and then have 'wilfully' and deliberately fallen away.

[1] S. John xv. 4, 5; xiv. 23; Rom. viii. 10; Eph. iii. 17; Col. i. 27, etc.
[2] Heb. x. 26.   [3] Eph. iv. 21.

But, beloved, we are persuaded better things of you, and things that accompany salvation, though we thus speak: for God is not unrighteous to forget your work and the love which you showed towards His Name, in that ye ministered unto the saints, and still do minister. And we desire that each one of you may show the same diligence unto the fullness of hope even to the end: that ye be not sluggish, but imitators of them who through faith and patience inherit the promises.

The apostolic heart of the author reveals itself in the way in which, after so potent a warning, he at once seeks to reassure and encourage his readers, lest he should break the bruised reed or quench the smoking flax.[1]

'Things that belong unto salvation.' Salvation is of God, and is bestowed through the means He has appointed. But on man's side there must be the things which accompany, and bring about, his salvation: faith, repentance, hope, charity, good works, the use of the means of grace, etc.

So the Apostle bids the Philippians, 'Work out your own salvation with fear and trembling; for it is God Who worketh in you, both to will and to work for His good pleasure.'[2] 'God is not unrighteous,' that is, unjust.

'The love which you showed . . .' For 'faith worketh through love,' to God and one's neighbour.[3] 'What doth it profit, my brethren, if a man say he hath faith, but have no works? can that faith save him?'[4] No wonder that Luther, with his false doctrine of salvation by faith only, called the Epistle of S. James one 'of straw.'

'Sluggish,' dull in mind, lacking in zeal and perseverance.

'Imitators of them . . .' and especially of Abraham who believed the promise of God.

For when God made promise to Abraham, since He could swear by none greater, He sware by Himself, saying, Surely blessing I will bless thee, and multiplying I will multiply thee. And thus,

---

[1] Isa. xlii. 3.   [2] Phil. ii. 12.
[3] Gal. v. 6.   [4] S. Jas. ii. 14–26.

F

*having patiently endured, he obtained the promise. For men swear
by the greater: and in every dispute of theirs the oath is final for
confirmation. Wherein God, being minded to show more abundantly
unto the heirs of the promise the immutability of His counsel,
interposed with an oath: that by two immutable things, in which
it is impossible for God to lie, we may have a strong encouragement,
who have fled for refuge to lay hold of the hope set before us.*

The promise was made to Abraham and to his descendants.[1] Thus it had both an immediate, literal meaning,
and a spiritual one to be fulfilled in the future, both
conditional on faith and obedience. It was through faith
in God's promise that Isaac was born,[2] and the patriarchs
looked forward to the birth of the Messiah 'not having
received the promises, but having seen them afar off.'[3]
For as S. Paul says, 'Now to Abraham and his seed were
the promises made. He saith not, And to seeds, as of
many: but as of one, And to thy seed, which is Christ.'[4]
Thus whilst the promise primarily refers to temporal bless-
ings, its ultimate reference is to Christ and the Gospel,
and so to the faithful, of whom Abraham is the father.[5]

The writer goes on to remind his readers of the character
and finality of an oath solemnly made by men. By an
oath a man calls upon God to witness to the truth of the
statement he is about to make, and men accept this as a
proof that he is speaking the truth. He then applies this
to God, in accordance with many passages in the Old
Testament Scriptures.[6] God, in order to show that His
promises were not merely transitory, but permanent,
unchangeable ones, valid for the true heirs, the believers in Christ, confirmed them by swearing by Himself, since there existed no higher authority to whom
appeal might be made. Of course, and by necessity of the
fact that we can only speak in human language of divine
acts, the expression 'sware by Himself' does not mean

[1] Gen. xvii. 1–7; xxii. 17, 18.   [2] Heb. xi. 11, 12.   [3] ibid., xi. 13.
[4] Gal. iii. 16.   [5] Rom. iv. 11–13.
[6] Gen. xxvi. 3; Exod. xiii. 5, etc.; Deut. viii. 18; Ps. xcv. 11; S. Luke i. 73.

that God took an oath in the strict sense, for example, as
a man does. S. Ambrose comments, 'Since we commonly
regard as more true that which is confirmed by an oath,
lest our faith should halt, God is described as swearing,
though He does not actually do so' in a human manner.
Thus 'by two immutable' things, the promise and the
oath, 'in which it is impossible for God to lie,' impossible
because incompatible with His being God, the supreme
Truth, we are to be encouraged to endure patiently, and
withstand whatever temptations beset us who have already
by faith in Christ taken hold of the hope of eternal life
set before us.[1]

Which [hope] *we have as an anchor of the soul, a hope both
sure and steadfast and entering into that which is within the veil;
whither as a forerunner Jesus entered for us, having become a
high priest for ever after the order of Melchizedek.*

The theological virtue of hope differs from the hope
which is natural to man, and 'beats eternal in the human
breast,' in that it admits no doubt or uncertainty as is
implied in such sayings as, 'I hope it will be fine to-
morrow,' or 'I shall hope to see you again.' For it is
centred in God, in His mercy, His promises, and His
power; and just as by faith we make real to ourselves
what is eternally real and existent, so that they abide
within us, so by hope we already lay hold of, and are
possessed by, eternal life itself. In the phrase, 'entering into
that which is within the veil,' the same truth is expressed
by reference to the veil which separated the 'Holy Place'
from the 'Holy of holics,' the innermost shrine of the
Tabernacle and the Temple.[2] The true 'Holy of holies'
is heaven, into which our hope enters with Jesus Who as
our High Priest and Forerunner has gone before to prepare
a place for us.[3]

We come now to the central part of the Epistle in which

[1] Cf. Col. i. 5; Tit. ii. 13.   [2] Heb. ix. 1–7.   [3] S. John xiv. 2.

the author demonstrates the superiority of the Priesthood
of Jesus to that of the Levitical priesthood.

*For this Melchizedek, King of Salem, priest of God Most
High, who met Abraham returning from the slaughter of the
kings, and blessed him, to whom also Abraham divided a tenth
part of all* [the booty], *(being first, by interpretation, King of
righteousness, and then also King of Salem, which is King of
peace: without father, without mother, without genealogy, having
neither beginning of days nor end of life, but made like unto the
Son of God, abideth a priest continually.*

The account of this meeting between Abraham and
Melchizedek is given in Genesis xiv. 18–20. Much specula-
tion has been expended on the question as to who this
priest-king was, of whom such strange things are said.
The most likely explanation is that he was a Canaanitish
king of Jerusalem who was also a priest of the God Whom
Abraham worshipped. This seems clear from the fact that
Abraham is blessed by him, and renders him a tenth of
the spoils taken from the kings, according to the custom
of the time. The statement that he was 'without father
. . . genealogy . . .' etc., simply means that nothing of his
forebears or pedigree, or of his end, is known to the writer
of Genesis. This fact is emphasized in contrast to the law
by which the Levitical priests were compelled to show
their pedigree, or 'family tree,' since the priestly office
descended from father to son, and the high priest must be
able to establish his claim to be of Aaron's line.

The writer, then, uses the phrases 'without father,' etc.,
not in the sense of 'fatherless' or 'deathless,' but only that
none of these facts are recorded in the Scriptures. This
sense is common in both Greek and Latin writers. Philo of
Alexandria calls Sarah 'motherless,' because her mother's
name is not mentioned; Livy and Horace use similar terms;
and the Jewish Rabbis say, 'The Gentile has no father,'
meaning that he has no Jewish pedigree.

As Melchizedek thus appears in the Scriptures, so is
Christ in actual fact without beginning or end, since He
is the eternal Word Who from all eternity 'was with God,
and was God,' as has been shown in chapter i. Of the
human nature which He assumed we have both its beginning at Nazareth, and its pedigree,[1] and know it to be
without end.

The author of Hebrews uses the story for one purpose
only, that is, to establish the fact that before the Law,
and the Aaronic priesthood, there was a priesthood,
recognized by Abraham, which confirmed the blessing
and the promises made by God to him, 'Blessed be Abram
of the Most High God, possessor of heaven and earth.'
This kingly priesthood of justice and peace is a type and
figure of our Lord's kingly and priestly office, one not
derived from Aaron but directly from God Himself. It is
in line with that of Melchizedek, and greater and more
effectual than that of Aaron which no more annulled it
than the Law annulled the promises made to Abraham,
and through him to all believers.[2]

The concluding phrase, 'abideth a priest continually,'
does not mean 'for ever,' but 'so long as he lived,' and
hints that his priesthood was unique in that there is no
record of his having any successor.

*Now consider how great this man was, unto whom Abraham,
the patriarch, gave a tenth of the chief spoils. And they indeed
of the sons of Levi that receive the priest's office have commandment
to take tithes of the people according to the Law, that is, of their
brethren, though these have come out of the loins of Abraham: but
he whose genealogy is not counted from them hath taken tithes of
Abraham, and hath blessed him that hath the promises. But without any dispute the less is blessed of the greater. And here, men
that die receive tithes; but there one, of whom it is witnessed that
he liveth. And, so to say, through Abraham even Levi, who*

---

[1] S. Matt. i; S. Luke iii. 23.   [2] Cf. Rom. iv. 13–17; Gal. iii. 6–22.

receiveth tithes, hath paid tithes; for he was yet in the loins of his father when Melchizedek met him.

The whole argument of this passage is designed to show in what lay the superiority of the priesthood of Melchizedek. This lay in the facts that Abraham paid tithes to him, that he blessed Abraham, and that, unlike the priests of the Law who die, 'he liveth.' Each of these facts would have a much greater significance to Jewish readers than to Gentiles, and so to modern readers. For to the former tithe was a religious tax, the idea of which is derived from that of possession, and the symbolism of the number 10.

Possession includes a number of things, and the decade, which contains all the figures of which all numbers consist, is a symbol of all property which can be numbered. Thus, to give a tenth of one's possessions to God was regarded as an acknowledgement that the whole was owed to Him. Such a tithe gave the whole a religious character, a consecration, which untithed property did not share. From this belief arose the custom of rendering a tithe of spoils taken in war and thus, as it were, legitimizing it as the possession of the captor. Now the Levitical priesthood received the tithes of all the descendants of their common father, Abraham. But he had himself paid tithe to one who was not of that priesthood; and indeed it might be said that even the Levites had paid tithe to Melchizedek, inasmuch as they were of the same stock, being the posterity of Abraham. This would be more keenly realized by those whose sense of racial and tribal unity was so much stronger than ours is, even after the truth of the solidarity of the human race has been impressed upon us by two wars.

The second link in the argument consists in the fact that Abraham, the blessed of God, receives the blessing of Melchizedek who is thus revealed as greater than Abraham. Further, a formal, priestly blessing is more than a mere wishing of good, it actually bestows what it

expresses, and does so because God has empowered men
to do what, in the strictest sense, He alone can do. Herein
lies the sanction by which Melchizedek blesses Abraham
as 'priest of the Most High God,' and is shown to be
greater than Abraham.

The third link is the contrast between the Levitical
priests, who succeed each other by natural generation,
and pass away by death, with Melchizedek who, 'as it
might be said,' liveth for ever. The Greek phrase implies
that the statement is not to be taken literally, and should
be translated in the above sense. Holy Scripture, so the
writer would seem to argue, does not record the birth or
death of Melchizedek, as it does of the priests of the Law,
so that it may be said that his priesthood lives on as a
reality in the supernatural order, and comes into actual
being in Christ, Who did not belong to the priestly tribe
of Levi, but to that of Judah, so that 'after the likeness of
Melchizedek there ariseth another priest, who is made so,
not after the law of a carnal [that is, natural] commandment, but after the power of an endless life.'[1]

*Now if there was perfection through the Levitical priesthood
(for under it hath the people received the Law), what further need
was there that another priest should arise after the order of
Melchizedek, and not be reckoned after the order of Aaron?*

The perfection spoken of is the bringing of man to
the end for which he was created, and which our Lord
bids him seek. 'Be perfect, even as your Father Who is in
heaven is perfect.'[2] This does not meant that we shall
be perfect in the unique manner in which God is perfection itself, but after our own human manner, perfected
human beings. Such perfection, if sought for during our
earthly life, will be consummated in heaven, where, as
S. John says, we shall be like God 'for we shall see Him
as He is.'[3] The belief in such a perfecting vision of God

[1] verses 14–16.   [2] S. Matt. v. 48. Cf. Eph. iii. 19; Phil. iii. 12, etc.
[3] 1 S. John iii. 2.

was common to the highest Jewish and pagan thought, as was also the conviction that only the man of a disciplined, evil-renouncing, holiness-desiring life could attain it. Both Jew and pagan recognized, too, that the first need of man was to be rid of the sin which lay between him and God, and separated him from God. For this some form of mediation between God and man was necessary, hence the priesthood in which one man was chosen to represent the whole community in its approach to God, and sacrifice by which man not only acknowledged God as his supreme Lord, but also admitted his sinfulness for which some atonement and reparation must be made. But great as was the symbolic value of the ancient sacrifices, they were no more than symbols; they did not bestow what they symbolized. And men had come to realize this: the whole known world lay under the sense of its own impotence and sin, through which there flickered gleams of a hope, almost a premonition, that a deliverer was at hand.

For the priesthood being changed, there is made of necessity a change in the Law. For He of Whom these things are said belongeth to another tribe, from which no man hath given attendance at the altar. For it is evident that our Lord hath sprung out of Judah; as to which tribe Moses spake nothing concerning priests. And what we say is yet more abundantly evident, if after the likeness of Melchizedek there ariseth another priest, who hath been made, not after the law of a carnal commandment, but after the power of an endless life; for it is witnessed of Him,

    Thou art a priest for ever
    After the order of Melchizedek.

The ancient Law centred round the priesthood whose duty was to see that it was obeyed, and to fulfil its highest functions. Thus a change in the priesthood, by which it was brought to an end, involved a change in the Law. And that the former had been changed was evident from the fact that our Lord was not of the tribe of Levi, but of that of Judah, from which no priest was taken. The Jews themselves admitted that the Messiah Who is spoken of in Psalm cx was to be of David's line, and were non-plussed when Jesus asked, 'How, then, doth David in the Spirit call Him Lord, saying,

> The Lord said unto my Lord,
> Sit Thou on My right hand,
> Till I put Thine enemies beneath My feet?[1]

And that Jesus was the Messiah was a cardinal point in the apostolic belief and preaching.[2]

For there is a disannulling of a foregoing commandment because of its weakness and unprofitableness (for the Law made nothing perfect), and a bringing in thereupon of a better hope, through which we draw near to God. And inasmuch as it is not without the taking of an oath (for they indeed have been made priests without an oath; but He with an oath by Him that said of Him,

> *The Lord sware and will not repent Himself*
> *Thou art a priest for ever);*

by so much also hath Jesus become the surety of a better covenant.

The commandment which went before is that concerning the institution of the Levitical priesthood which was only a temporary, educative provision designed as a fore-runner and type of that 'better hope' by which we may truly 'draw nigh to God.' Both the Law and the Levitical priesthood had its work to do, but neither was able actually to take away sin, nor to bestow that grace which man needed to perfect his nature.[3] Writing to the Romans, S. Paul says that 'the Law is holy, and the commandment holy, and righteous, and good.' By it sin was shown to be sinful and its issue moral and spiritual death. But it could not free men from sin, nor enable them to overcome the lower part of their nature forever 'warring against the law of' their minds.[4] For 'what,

---

[1] S. Matt. xxii. 41–46.   [2] Acts ii. 22–36; iii. 18–21, etc.
[3] Cf. Heb. ix. 9, 10; x. 1, 2.   [4] Rom. vii. 7–25.

then, is the Law? It was added because of transgressions, till the seed should come to whom the promise [made to Abraham] hath been made. . . . If there had been a Law given which could make alive, truly righteousness would have been of the Law.'[1] To make alive, that is what it could not do, for 'the righteous shall live by faith'; and the Law is not of faith.[2] It is an external command calling for an external obedience, not a power enabling men to be obedient. Or like the slave whose duty it was to see a boy safely to school, so was it meant to bring the Jews unto Christ.[3]

'By so much more . . .': that is, by the facts already related, is our Lord's Priesthood so much greater than that of the Law, and He is the surety or guarantee of a better and enduring Covenant, one which He has Himself established in His own Person, and Who as the Eternal Priest having entered into heaven as Man, and for men, is 'the faithful witness'[4] to, and surety of, God's New Covenant with man.

And they indeed have been made priests many in number, because that by death they are hindering from continuing: but He, because He abideth for ever, hath His Priesthood unchangeable. Wherefore also He is able to save to the uttermost them that draw near unto God through Him, seeing He ever liveth to make intercession for them.

The Levitical priesthood was of a physical, mechanical succession; that of our Lord is one of spiritual, undying life and power. The words, 'hath His Priesthood unchangeable,' may be taken to mean, that Christ's Priesthood is not transmitted to successors, or that it is immutable and imperishable. The former meaning cannot be used as an argument against the Catholic priesthood as this consists of a sharing in the spiritual authority and power of our Lord's priestly life and act. What is known

---

[1] Gal. iii. 19, 21.   [2] ibid., iii. 11.
[3] ibid., iv. 24.   [4] Rev. i. 5.

as the 'apostolic succession' is not *merely* an outward, mechanical link with apostolic practice, a visible guarantee of the right possessed by their legitimate successors to act as Apostles. The essence of the Sacrament of Holy Order consists in the fact that it is an effectual sign which actually confers the grace signified by deed and word, a grace not, as it were, passed down from a remote past through a succession of bishops, but directly conferred by God through those who now possess an apostolic authority. Moreover, the Christian priest does not so much act *for* Christ as *in* Christ, or as S. Thomas says: 'It is Christ Who baptizes, He Himself Who remits sins; He, the true Priest, Who offered Himself upon the altar of the Cross and by Whose power His Body and Blood are daily consecrated on the altar.'[1]

The doctrine of the Catholic priesthood must be seen in the light of that of the Church as the living Body of Christ of which each individual member continues the life of Christ in his or her particular vocation. So the priest, as priest, continues on earth that eternal and immutable Priesthood now enshrined in heaven. We are not claiming that this was in the writer's mind, but only that his words cannot be taken as containing any meaning such as would tell against the Church's teaching. All that he is concerned with is the nature of the Priesthood of our Lord Himself in contrast to that of the Levitical priesthood. It is, he continues, because the former is unchangeable that 'He is able to save to the uttermost,' that is, fully, completely, 'those that draw near unto God through Him' Who has declared: 'I am the Way,' and 'No man cometh unto the Father but by Me.'[2]

It does not seem unnecessary to point out that both in our Lord's teaching and in that of His Apostles it is God 'Who is the Trinity,' to use Augustine's phrase, Who is the Centre and the End of all Christian faith, devotion,

---

[1] *Summa contra Gentiles*, iv. 76.   [2] S. John xiv. 6.

and life. We are to come to Christ as the Door[1] by
which we enter the Way by being made one with
Him Who is the Way, the Way to be followed and
lived, the Way of conformity to the divine will which
He ever fulfilled,[2] and alone enables us to fulfil. As
the Way in His sacred humanity He has reached that
End which we have still to seek and attain, by 'a new
and living way, that is to say, His flesh,'[3] in the knowledge that there, in the centre of heaven's secure and
inviolable Majesty, 'He ever liveth to make intercession
for us.'

But in what way, by what means, does He thus inter-
cede for us? To answer this question we must rid our
minds of modern ideas about intercession with the
practices which have resulted from them, such as 'intercession papers,' 'intercession services,' etc., and see what
the word meant to the writer. In Hebrew, Greek, and
Aramaic it was used of any drawing near to God, and
continued to be used in the same sense in English up to
the seventeenth century. It also implied the idea of
sacrifice, and both meanings are to be understood in the
sentence before us. Our Lord's intercession in heaven is
not one of words, or of the enumeration of various
objects, but the presentation of Himself as 'the Lamb
once slain,' in the presence of God. For just as He is the
one true Worshipper and Worship, so is He the one
Interceder and Intercession. And what He is in heaven,
that is He in the Mass by which His worship and intercession is, as it were, placed in our hands that we may be
lifted up, and become part of it. To substitute 'intercession services' for the one great interceding act of our Lord
is but one of the many ways in which men prefer anything
rather than simple obedience to our Lord's command,
'Do this,' by which we, His Body on earth, 'show forth
the Lord's death till He come.'[4]

[1] ibid., x. 9.   [2] S. John v. 30, etc.
[3] Heb. x. 20.   [4] 1 Cor. xi. 26.

*For such a high priest became us, holy, guileless, undefiled,
separated from sinners, and made higher than the heavens; who
needeth not daily, like those high priests, to offer up sacrifices, first
for his own sins, and then for those of the people: for this He
did once for all, when He offered up Himself. For the Law
appointeth men high priests, having infirmity; but the word of the
oath, which was after the Law, appointeth a Son, perfected for
evermore.*

'Such a high priest became us,' that is, was such as we
needed owing to our weak and sinful condition. One not
only, as we have seen, eternal, all powerful, veritable Son
of God, but also one Who though incarnate 'in the likeness
of sinful flesh,'[1] was yet holy in the highest moral sense of
the term; guileless, 'Who did no sin, neither was guile
found in His mouth';[2] undefiled in mind and body;
separated from sinners, both during His earthly life in
which He mixed with them, but was not one of them, and
now in His heavenly state. Such a high priest does not
need, as did the Jewish priests, to offer daily sacrifices
which could not take away sins, since He has offered
Himself once for all men upon the Cross, and eternally
presents His Sacrifice in heaven as an abiding, ever-
efficacious act for the redemption of the world; which
Sacrifice His Church offers on earth in the Mass, which
is the sacramental representation of that Sacrifice in the
temporal order.

The writer's statement, as it stands, has nothing to
do with the daily Sacrifice of the Mass, it refers only
to the Old Testament sacrifices, and to the one Sacrifice
of Christ which He, in His own Person, offered on Calvary
and now pleads in heaven. His words, therefore, cannot
be used as an argument against the daily Masses of the
Church, which are not a series of different, or additional
sacrifices, but Christ's one, eternal Sacrifice shown forth
by, and in, His Body on earth.

[1] Rom. viii. 3; cf. Phil. ii. 7.   [2] 1 S. Pet. ii. 22.

Now to sum up what we are saying, the chief point is this: We have such a High Priest, Who sat down on the right hand of the throne of the Majesty in the heavens, a minister of the sanctuary, and of the true tabernacle, which the Lord pitched, not man.

All that has been said about the High Priesthood of Christ is summed up in the fact that we Christians have a heavenly High Priest, one Who has taken His rightful place in heaven where, in the true sanctuary and tabernacle, of which that which Moses commanded to be made for use in the wilderness, was a symbol and foreshadowing, He ministers that Sacrifice which He offered on earth. The word 'true' is used here, not in opposition to 'false,' but to what is imperfect and temporary, as was the earthly tabernacle, a contrast heightened by the following phrase, 'which the Lord pitched' abidingly, not as the Israelites pitched the tabernacle tent at successive resting-places on the trek from Egypt to the promised land.

For every high priest is appointed to offer both gifts and sacrifices: wherefore it is necessary that this High Priest also have somewhat to offer. Now if He were on earth, He would not be a priest at all, seeing there are those who offer the gifts according to the Law; who serve that which is a copy and shadow of the heavenly things, even as Moses is warned of God when he is about to make the tabernacle; for, See, saith He, that thou make all things according to the pattern that was showed thee in the mount.

The chief function of priesthood is the offering of sacrifice. If Christ, then, is a High Priest He must have some sacrifice to offer, and some place in which to offer. Now since He does not belong to the priestly tribe of Levi, but to that of Judah, from which no priest is chosen under the Law, and moreover there are such priests still ministering in the Temple, He Himself does not now act in Person as a priest on earth, as He did on Calvary when He offered the Sacrifice of Himself in Person once for all. This does not imply that there is now no priesthood or sacrifice on earth, where, on the contrary, both exist and function. For in the Eucharist He does not offer His Sacrifice in Person, it is the Church, His Body, which does so by His command.

The account of the revelation made by God to Moses concerning the tabernacle may be found in Exodus xxv and following chapters. That revelation, like those made to S. John and recorded by him in the Apocalypse, was of an intellectual and spiritual nature, the content of which could only be described in human language, and executed in earthly materials. The vision of 'heavenly things,' seen by the eyes of the mind, and destined to be copied in material form, is given in order that there may be on earth a place and a manner in which man, a creature of body no less than soul, should be able to approach God consciously and corporately, and also be prepared to receive a more perfect revelation of which the tabernacle with its priesthood and sacrifices was but a foreshadowing. In all this we may see how God deals with man, as with all His creatures, according to his nature, that of a being who acquires all his knowledge through his bodily senses, and can only approach, worship, and serve God by using his body.

There is no such thing for man as 'a purely spiritual' religion. The divine and eternal realities which are the essence of religion lie beyond the reach of the senses, and can only be known by man as they are conveyed to him under the physical means of words, events, symbolic of, and, in Christianity, actually conferring, that which they symbolize. The latter is as 'anthropomorphic' as was Judaism, if not more so, since it tells of God assuming, and dwelling on earth, not under a symbol, as was the *Shekinah*, the cloud of glory overshadowing the mercy-seat, but in man's very nature.

But now hath He obtained a ministry the more excellent, by how much also He is the Mediator of a better covenant which hath

*been enacted upon better promises. For if that first Covenant had
been faultless, then would no place have been sought for a second.
For finding fault with them, He saith,*

> *Behold, the days come, saith the Lord,*
> *That I will make a New Covenant with the house of Israel and
>   with the house of Judah;*
> *Not according to the Covenant that I made with their fathers*
> *In the day that I took them by the hand to lead them forth out
>   of the land of Egypt;*
> *For they continued not in My Covenant,*
> *And I regarded them not, saith the Lord.*
> *For this is the Covenant that I will make with the house of
>   Israel*
> *After those days, saith the Lord;*
> *I will put My laws into their mind,*
> *And on their hearts also will I write them:*
> *And I will be to them a God,*
> *And they shall be to Me a people;*
> *And they shall not teach every man his fellow-citizen,*
> *And every man his brother, saying, Know the Lord;*
> *For all shall know Me,*
> *From the least to the greatest of them.*
> *For I will be merciful to their iniquities,*
> *And their sins will I remember no more.*

*In that He saith, A New Covenant, He hath made the first old.
But that which is becoming old and waxeth aged is nigh unto
passing away.*

The ministry of Christ surpasses both that of Moses
and of Aaron, the former the mediator of the Law,[1] the
latter the chief representative of the ancient priesthood.
Christ as the divinely-appointed kingly High Priest is
now the 'One Mediator between God and men,'[2] the
Revealer and Mediator of the New Covenant which rests
upon those 'better promises' already spoken of. Such a
New Covenant was necessary because of the defects in
that made by God through Moses. Those defects were:

[1] Gal. iii. 19. [2] 1 Tim. ii. 5.

(1) That it rested upon certain conditions to be fulfilled by those with whom it was made.[1] The promises of God were bound up with the obligations laid upon the Hebrew people. If they did not fulfil them God was no longer bound to fulfil His promises. And the whole of the Old Testament is a record of their repeated failure to do so.

(2) It was insufficient in that it did not do more than provide an external Law which of itself it did not enable men to fulfil. Saul the Pharisee, 'exceedingly jealous for the traditions of my fathers,'[2] came to experience the impotency of the Law which, whilst it revealed the sinfulness of sin, could not take away sin, or make anything perfect.[3]

(3) It was a transitory, impermanent thing, a mere copy which did not effectually reproduce the grace and power of the original; the shadow of a real good which was to come, a preparatory school whose object was to make men realize their need, and to prepare them to recognize, and receive its fulfilment when it should come. It was a means to an end by which it should be fulfilled, and Christ was that End and Fulfilment.[4] This was no new truth but one reiterated by the prophets to whom the writer refers in the opening words of his Epistle, and of which he now reminds his readers.

By the mouth of Jeremiah[5] God had made known His intention to make a New Covenant with His people, one unlike that which He had made of old, and which was still in force. This was a written Law imposed upon men from without calling for an external, legally conceived obedience. But the New Covenant was to be of an inward, spiritual character written in the minds and hearts of men, not merely on tables of stone, the doorposts of their houses, or on parchments bound upon wrist and forehead.[6] Such a New Covenant implied, and indeed brought about, the end of that old one which was already

---

[1] Deut. xxix.   [2] Gal. i. 14.
[3] Rom. vii. 7–24; Heb. vii. 19; ix. 9–10.   [4] Rom. x. 4; S. Matt. v. 17.
[5] Jer. xxxi. 31 ff.   [6] Deut. vi. 8, 9; cf. 2 Cor. iii. 3.

G

nearing decay and death, was but an empty shell devoid of any living power, a teacher who could only go on reciting lessons which did not touch the hearts or heal the consciences of men.

Now even the first Covenant had ordinances of divine worship, and its sanctuary of the world. For there was a tabernacle prepared, the first, wherein were the candlestick, the table, and the shewbread; which is called the Holy Place. And after the second veil, the tabernacle which is called the Holy of holies; having a golden censer, and the ark of the Covenant overlaid round about with gold, wherein was a golden pot holding the manna, and Aaron's rod that budded, and the tables of the Covenant; and above it cherubim of glory overshadowing the mercy-seat; of which things we cannot now speak severally.

Nor, indeed, was he concerned about them since they added nothing to his argument. He seems to have mentioned these particular furnishings and contents from memory, and with no more purpose than to accentuate the preliminary statement that there was a sanctuary upon earth designed for the worship of God. A detailed account of the construction and contents of the tabernacle may be found in Exodus xxv–xxvii. Of those mentioned here[1] the candlestick was a seven-branched one rising from a massive base.

'The table' on which the shewbread was placed, the latter being twelve loaves of fine flour,[2] which were renewed weekly.

'The censer,' or 'altar of incense,' used in the daily services.[3]

'The ark of the Covenant,' in which was placed a gold vessel containing some of the manna with which the people were fed in the wilderness;[4] Aaron's rod which blossomed;[5] and the two tables of the Law.[6] Above the

---

[1] Exod. xxv. 21–26. A relief on the Arch of Titus depicts its being borne through the streets of Rome after the final fall of Jerusalem in A.D. 70.

[2] Lev. xxiv. 5–7.   [3] Exod. xxx. 7, 8.

[4] Exod. xvi. 33, 34.   [5] Num. xvii. 5, 7.   [6] Deut. x. 1–5.

ark was the mercy-seat, at each side of which was a
golden cherub, each facing the other, their outstretched
wings overshadowing the mercy-seat, where God had
promised to meet with Moses, and communicate His will
to him.[1]

But what was of importance to the author's argument
was the arrangement of the actual tabernacle, which was
an elaborate tent standing in the centre of a large open
space surrounded by a wall of curtains. Within this
tabernacle were two chambers; the first, known as the
Holy Place, before which hung a curtain or veil; the
second, the Holy of holies, separated from the Holy Place
by another veil.[2]

*Now these things having been thus prepared, the priests go in
continually into the first tabernacle* [that is, the Holy Place],
accomplishing the [daily] *services; but into the second* [that is,
the Holy of holies] *the high priest alone, once in the year, not
without blood, which he offereth for himself, and for the errors of
the people: the Holy Ghost thus signifying that the way into the
Holy Place* [here meaning the Holy of holies as typifying
heaven] *hath not yet been made manifest, while as the first
tabernacle is yet standing: which is a parable for the time now
present; according to which are offered both gifts and sacrifices
that cannot, as touching the conscience, make the worshipper perfect, being only (with meats and drinks and divers washings)
carnal ordinances imposed until a time of reformation.*

The whole point of the foregoing paragraph lies in the
fact that no one except the high priest, and he only on
one day of the year, the great Day of Atonement, was
permitted to enter the Holy of holies, the innermost
shrine of the tabernacle. For this was the nearest approach
of heaven to earth, over which hung the cloud of glory,
the *Shekinah*, the visible witness to God's abiding presence
with His people.[3] Into this awe-filled shrine, its silent

---

[1] Exod. xxv. 17-22.   [2] ibid.. xxvi. 31-36.   [3] ibid., xl. 34-38.

mystery undisturbed by human foot or voice, one man
alone dare enter once a year on his own behalf, and on
that of the people whom he could not take with him.
Thus did the Holy Spirit ever remind the people of God
of that gate of heaven closed by the sin of man, of their
need of a mediator, and of the cleansing and consecrating
blood without which even the high priest must not come
into the divine presence of the All-Holy God. So long as
that tabernacle, and the Temple which later took its
place, was standing, it remained as an open, manifest
sign that the way to the heaven of which it was a symbol
was still closed to men.

Now it was, claims our author, the Holy Ghost Who
illuminated the mind of Moses to construct the tabernacle, and to arrange the ceremonies so that they symbolized heavenly realities. It was not a new conception
of the activity of the Holy Ghost, it is found in Exodus xxxi
where God says of Bezaleel, whom He had called to
execute the elaborate workmanship which adorned the
tabernacle, 'I have filled him with the Spirit of God, in
wisdom, and in understanding, and in knowledge, and
in all manner of workmanship.'[1]

Thus the whole of the tabernacle and its services was
'a parable,' an outward expression of, and reference to,
divine mysteries which were to be made known in 'the
time now present,' that is, of the Christian dispensation.

'According to which' parable of the earthly tabernacle,
with its sacrifices and accompanying ceremonies and
offerings, nothing could be perfected, since they were but
outward bodily ordinances imposed as a preparation for
the coming time when all should be reformed by being
fulfilled by Christ to Whom they pointed.

But Christ having come a High Priest of the good things to
come, through the greater and more perfect tabernacle, not made

[1] Cf. Isa. xi. 2 and S. Augustine's praise of God, 'because those beautiful
patterns which through men's souls are conveyed into their cunning hands
come from that Beauty, which is above our souls' (*Confessions*, x. 34).

with hands, that is to say, not of this creation, nor yet through the
blood of goats and calves, but through His own Blood, entered in
once for all into the holy place, having obtained eternal redemption.

The good things typified by the Hebrew tabernacle
have now come to pass in and through the sacred humanity of the divine Word, that 'greater and more perfect
tabernacle not made with hands,' but 'conceived by the
Holy Ghost, born of the Virgin Mary.' The fact of our
Lord's Priesthood derives from that of the Incarnation,
since it is only as He is the Word made flesh, God and
man in one Person, that He becomes such a High Priest as
is needed to accomplish man's redemption. And not only
Priest but Victim Who 'through His own Blood,' that
is, the offering of His own life, 'having obtained eternal
redemption' has also entered into the true Holy of holies,
'heaven itself,'[1] in that human nature in which He is for
ever both the Priest and Victim of our salvation.

For if the blood of goats and bulls, and the ashes of a heifer
sprinkling them that have been defiled, sanctify unto the cleanness
of the flesh: how much more shall the Blood of Christ, Who
through the eternal Spirit offered Himself without blemish unto
God, cleanse your conscience from dead works to serve the living
God?

An account of the ceremonies here mentioned will be
found in Leviticus xvi and Numbers xix. These were
concerned only with breaches of the Law, and only
affected the relation of the individual, or community, to
it. They sanctified, not in the Christian, but in a legal
sense only, by removing the ceremonial uncleanness con-
tracted by some offence against the Law. They did not
cleanse the conscience, or make holy, 'perfect,' the worshipper. Yet, argues the writer, if they could and did
restore men to a ceremonial cleanliness in which they
might take part in the worship of the tabernacle, 'how

[1] Cf. Heb. ix. 24.

much more' shall the Blood of Christ cleanse the innermost soul from sin.

To offer one's blood is to offer oneself, as when we say of a man, 'He gave his life for his comrades,' or 'He shed his blood for them.'

The phrase 'who through the eternal Spirit' is capable of two interpretations. (i) Who by the guidance and inspiration of the Holy Ghost Who dwelt in the human nature of Christ.[1] (ii) It may mean the Godhead of our Lord,[2] and so points to the truth that it was His divinity which gave His Sacrifice an infinite value.

And for this cause He is the Mediator of a New Covenant, that a death having taken place for the redemption of the transgressions that were under the first Covenant, they that have been called may receive the promise of the eternal inheritance.

The Greek word usually translated by the English 'covenant' also means 'testament, will, legacy,' as in this sentence, and in the Gospel accounts of the Institution of the Eucharist. Christ has offered Himself upon the Cross for us, and because of this, by virtue of this death He is the Mediator of a new testament, by which He bequeathes to those who are called to faith in Him an eternal inheritance. Of this inheritance the Christian is already a partaker, having received 'the adoption of sons.'[3]

For where a testament is there must of necessity be the death of him who made it. For a testament is of force where there hath been death; for it doth never avail while he that made it liveth. Wherefore even the first Covenant hath not been dedicated without blood. For when every commandment had been spoken by Moses to all the people, he took the blood of the calves and the goats, with water and scarlet wool and hyssop, and sprinkled both the book

---

[1] S. John iii. 34; S. Luke iii. 22, etc.
[2] As in Rom. i. 4, and 1 Tim. iii. 16.   [3] Gal. iv. 5.

itself, and all the people, saying, This is the blood of the Covenant which God commanded to you-ward. Moreover the tabernacle and all the vessels of the ministry he sprinkled in like manner with blood. And according to the Law, I may almost say, all things are cleansed with blood, and apart from shedding of blood there is no remission.

It is the death of Christ which makes the new testament effective for men. The Precious Blood, which is the very life of Christ poured forth upon the Cross, becomes our redemption and salvation, since it is not only given for us, but also given to us, Blood of the living Christ by Whose life once offered for us we are now saved.[1]

It was necessary, therefore, that the copies of the things in the heavens should be cleansed with these; but the heavenly things themselves with better things than these.

Necessary, not on the part of God, Who cannot be necessitated by anything outside Himself, but on account of, and following from, the typical character of the ancient Mosaic ceremonies, which were copies of heavenly things. The latter half of the sentence provokes the question, How could heavenly things require cleansing? If we refer to the account given in Exodus xxiv of the reading of the Law and the consequent sprinkling of blood upon the altar and people, two things seem to be clear. First, that this sprinkling of blood is an outward sign of the Covenant which God made with His people, and of their dedication of themselves, made in their response, 'All that the Lord hath said will we do and be obedient.' And secondly, what our author goes on to say of the sprinkling of blood in general, which is not derived from the passage quoted, refers only to the tabernacle as a whole, and to the various things used in the services.[2] Only on one occasion, that of the great Day of Atonement, is blood brought into the Holy of holies, and this, not to cleanse

---

[1] Rom. v. 9, 10.   [2] Cf. Num. xix. 18.

it, but the high priest himself, his household, and the people.[1] The whole idea is that of 'reconciling the Holy Place,' not in itself (for how could that which was help to be God's dwelling-place on earth need cleansing or reconciliation?), but the ceremonial removing of the barrier of sin which prevented immediate entrance into the divine Presence.

Thus, in figure, but no more, was the way opened, and the people reconciled to God. All this prefigured such a true cleansing and dedication, both of men and of things concerned with the worship of God, as was made by the 'blood of sprinkling'[2] by which 'we have been sanctified through the offering of the Body of Jesus Christ once for all,'[3] and 'have boldness to enter into the [true] holy place by the Blood of Jesus, by the way which He hath dedicated for us, a new and living way.'[4]

Thus 'heavenly things' does not refer to heaven itself, but to the worshippers who need such cleansing, and to all the means and things which the Church uses in her approach to, and worship of, God. That they need cleansing with 'better sacrifices' than those of the Mosaic dispensation is because the latter were only external, legalistic rites which could not touch and heal the conscience, nor serve to admit the worshipper into the Holy of holies, whilst the latter bear a sacramental character, effecting what they signify in those who use them in faith, and so 'draw near with a true heart in fullness of faith, having our hearts sprinkled from an evil conscience, and our bodies washed with pure water.'[5] They derive their efficacy from the fact that—

Christ entered not into a holy place made with hands, like in pattern to the true; but into heaven itself, now to appear before the face of God for us; nor yet that He should offer Himself often; as the high priest entered into the Holy Place year by year with blood

[1] Lev. xvi. 15–20.   [2] Heb. xii. 24.   [3] ibid., x. 19.
                    [4] ibid., x. 20.   [5] ibid., x. 22.

not his own; else must He often have suffered since the foundation of the world: but now once at the end of the ages hath He been manifested to put away sin by the Sacrifice of Himself.

Our Lord frequented the Temple in Jerusalem[1] but never passed the veil which hung before the Holy Place wherein the Jewish priests alone might tread, nor do we read of Him offering any of the accustomed personal sacrifices. His Priesthood and Sacrifice were fulfilled in the Upper Room and on Calvary, His oblation of Himself being made on Maundy Thursday night, and the immolation of Himself in His own Person, and with His own Blood, being consummated on Calvary. At this last moment 'the veil of the Temple was rent in the midst,'[2] as an outward sign of the removal of the barrier which men could not pass, and that the way into the true holy place, heaven itself, was now opened by the one Sacrifice of the Lamb of God Who taketh away the sins of the world.

That Sacrifice offered, and the certainty of the actual death established by the centurion's spear, and the taking down and burial of the Body, Christ rises from death and enters into His heavenly state of which the Ascension, some forty days later, is but an outward and visible sign.

'The end of the ages,' means the Christian era in contrast to the preceding ages of preparation for the coming of Christ. This is the last age in which God has 'spoken unto us by His Son,' and as S. John of the Cross

[1] This fact supplies an answer to the repeated assertion that our Lord only attended 'simple services,' and would not approve of such ceremonial practices as are common in the Catholic Church. On the contrary, so far as the Temple services were concerned, He never joined in any that were not of the most elaborate character. Nor did He express any disapproval of them, even when He insisted that the inward attitude of the worshipper was of primary importance. Nowhere in Holy Scripture is there any justification for the idea that a 'simple' service, like that of the synagogue, is more acceptable to God than an elaborate, ceremonial one like that of the Tabernacle and Temple. In fact, it is the latter which the Bible teaches is founded on a pattern of heavenly worship.

[2] S. Luke xxiii. 45.

says, 'has no more to say,' though His Church is always
learning more fully of the Faith 'once delivered unto the
saints.'[1]

*And inasmuch as it is appointed unto men once to die, and after
this cometh judgement; so Christ also, having been once offered to
bear the sins of many, shall appear a second time, apart from sin,
to them that wait for Him, unto salvation.*

The argument of this sentence is from the general to the
particular, as in 1 Corinthians xv. 12–17, where S. Paul
argues from the fact of the resurrection from the dead of
all men that Christ must have so risen. Here the fact that
all die and do not appear again until the general judgement is used to enforce the truth that so Christ, having
died, will appear again at the judgement, 'apart from sin,'
that is, not as atoning for sin, but as bringing salvation to
those who have believed in Him, and expect His return.

'Having been once offered to bear away the sins of
many.' Up to now the writer has emphasized the truth
that Christ offered Himself, and in the following chapter
he speaks of the voluntary character of that self-offering.[2]
So S. John records our Lord's words, 'I lay down My life,
that I may take it again. No one taketh it away from Me,
but I lay it down of Myself.'[3] But it is also true that His
death was brought about by men, by whom 'He is
brought as a lamb to the slaughter,'[4] and S. John tells us
how Caiaphas, being the high priest of that year, and as
holder of that sacred office, 'prophesied that Jesus should
die for the nation,' and adds, 'and not for the nation only,
but that He might also gather together the children of
God that are scattered abroad.'[5] Thus, as Claudel says
in *The Satin Slipper*, do 'all things minister to a Divine
Purpose, and so to one another, be it events or person-
alities. Even the falterings of circumstance and the
patternings of personality, sin and falsehood, are made

---

[1] S. Jude 3.   [2] Heb. x. 5–8.   [3] S. John x. 18.
          [4] Isa. liii. 7.   [5] S. John xi. 49–52.

to serve truth and justice, and above all, salvation in the long run.'

For the Law having a shadow of the good things to come, not the very image of the things, can never with the same sacrifices year by year, which they offer continually, make perfect them that draw nigh. Else would they not have ceased to be offered, because the worshippers, having been once cleansed, would have had no more conscience of sins? But in those sacrifices there is a remembrance made of sins year by year. For it is impossible that the blood of bulls and goats should take away sins.

The argument is continued and underlined by a repeated insistence upon the inadequate and transitory character of the Old as compared with the New Covenant. The former was but a shadow like that cast by, and deriving its being from, some object, or a mere vague outline the significance of which could only be discerned when it was filled in. Everything in it foreshadowed the good things of the Christian dispensation which, from the Old Testament point of view, were yet to come, it was not 'the very image' of those things. To understand the writer's use of the term 'image' it must be read in contrast to 'shadow.' Thus the word has the sense of 'unsubstantial' image or representation, as opposed to the 'true and substantial' image which, unlike the shadowed image, is the very substance of that which it represents. This image we know already; it is Christ, 'the very Image of' the substance of God,[1] Who contains within His own Person all that which He both represents and manifests to the world. The first part of the sentence has a parallel in S. Paul's reference to the feasts and customs of Judaism, 'which are a shadow of the things to come; but the body is Christ's.'[2] The sacrifices of the Law were signs only; not effectual signs, like the Christian Sacrifice and Sacraments which contain and

---

[1] Heb. i. 3; cf. 2 Cor. iv. 4; Col. i. 15; iii. 10.   [2] Col. ii. 16, 17.

accomplish what they signify. They did not remove the
consciousness of sin; on the contrary, they recalled it
year by year. Nor could they; how could the blood of
animals serve to take away sin, or to perfect him who
offered them?

> *Wherefore when He cometh into the world, He saith,*
> *Sacrifice and offering Thou wouldest not,*
> *But a body didst Thou prepare for Me;*
> *In whole burnt-offerings and sacrifices for sin Thou hadst*
> *   no pleasure:*
> *Then said I, Lo, I come*
> *(In the roll of the book it is written of Me)*
> *To do Thy will, O God.*

Saying above, Sacrifices and offerings and whole burnt-offerings
and sacrifices for sin Thou wouldest not, neither hadst pleasure
therein (the which are offered according to the Law), then hath
He said, Lo, I am come to do Thy will. He taketh away the
first, that He may establish the second.

In contrast to the sacrifices of animals not having any
will or choice of their own, we have the freely-chosen act
of the eternal Word and Son of God Who in the first
moment of His Incarnation, when He assumed that
human nature in which He was to redeem the world,
said, 'Lo, I come to do Thy will, O God.'

The quotation is from Psalm xl in which David recalls
the way in which God has aided him, and seeks for a more
adequate means of praising Him worthily than that of
outward sacrifices which, of themselves, have no value in
His sight. But 'in the roll of the book,' that is, the Book
of the Law, it is written that what God requires is man's
freewill offering of himself, the consequence of his having
the 'Law within his heart,' and thus exerting a moral
force, not merely an external, legal one.[1] Regarding
David's words as even more true of Christ, our writer uses

[1] Cf. Deut. vi. 4, 5; x. 12, etc.

them to express the deep, underlying motive which inspired the whole divine-human life of our Lord Who had
said, 'My meat is to do the will of Him that sent Me,'[1]
and, 'I seek not Mine own will, but the will of the Father
which sent Me.'[2] And that will was that He should be
the one Lamb of God,[3] Who should offer Himself as a
Sacrifice for the redemption of the world. 'The Son of
Man came . . . to give His life a ransom for many.'[4] That
Sacrifice, offered upon the Cross, and for ever unrepeat-
able, does away with all the sacrifices of the Law, in order
that it may be established as the one, abiding sacrifice of
the New Law, no longer offered by Christ in person as
upon Calvary, but by His Body, the Church, to whom
He committed the duty of that offering in His words:
'This is My Body which is broken for you: this do in
remembrance of Me.'[5]

*By which will we have been sanctified through the offering of
the Body of Christ once for all.*

'In which will,' rather than 'by which will.' The reference is to the will of the Father which our Lord made His
own, and accomplished, and so made our sanctification
possible. This first, by our being made members of Christ
in Baptism, in which we are both cleansed and made
holy that we may become holy in the fullest sense of
the word. For only as we are 'in Christ,' to use S. Paul's
repeated expression, by the free gift of His grace, can we
'grow in holiness' by our response to, and use of, that
grace.

And every [Jewish] *priest indeed standeth day by day ministering and offering oftentimes the same sacrifices, the which can never
take away sins: but He, when He had offered one sacrifice for
sins for ever, sat down on the right hand of God; from henceforth*

---

[1] S. John iv. 34.   [2] ibid., v. 30.   [3] ibid., i. 29.
          [4] S. Mark x. 45.   [5] i Cor. xi. 24.

expecting till His enemies be made the footstool of His feet. For by one offering He hath perfected for ever them that are sanctified.

The completeness and finality of our Lord's Sacrifice is stressed again by the contrast of the daily 'standing' of the Jewish priests to offer their ineffectual sacrifices with the 'sitting' of Christ Who, having accomplished His one Sacrifice, remains both priest and victim, although no longer offering His Sacrifice in Person.

'Them that are being sanctified,' indicates the process of sanctification in all who use the means by which the sanctifying grace of Calvary is applied to souls.

> *And the Holy Ghost also beareth witness to us: for after He hath said,*
> > *This is the Covenant that I will make with them*
> > *After those days, saith the Lord;*
> > *I will put My laws on their heart,*
> > *And upon their mind also will I write them;*
> *then saith He, And their sins and their iniquities will I remember no more. Now where remission of these is, there is no more offering for sin.*

The writer again quotes from Jeremiah xxxi, attributing the passage to its primary author. So he concludes the dogmatic section of his Epistle by claiming a divine sanction for its central thesis that Christ's Priesthood and Sacrifice has for ever abrogated that of the Mosaic Law.

The somewhat elaborate argument with its repetitions comes to an end, and the writer proceeds to state, and underline, the practical consequences which flow from it.

> *Having therefore, brethren, boldness to enter into the holy place by the Blood of Jesus, by the which He dedicated for us, a new and living way, through the veil, that is to say, His flesh:*

The true holy place is heaven itself but the full significance of the term will only be seen when we think of such passages of the New Testament as 'Our conversation is in heaven,'[1] that is, our present Christian manner of life; 'God has blessed us with every spiritual blessing in the heavenlies';[2] God hath 'raised us up with Christ, and made us to sit in the heavenlies in Christ Jesus';[3] 'Ye are come unto Mount Zion, and unto the city of the living God, the heavenly Jerusalem.'[4]

To be a Christian is to be one who has been admitted to a heavenly state, given access to heavenly things,[5] made a partaker of heavenly realities, one who is already 'in Christ,' a sharer in the divine life.[6] As our Lord entered into His heavenly glory at His Resurrection, so we at our Baptism 'that we may walk in newness of life,'[7] continuing, each one in his vocation, the life of Christ. And not His life alone, but also His office, for as S. John says, 'He hath made us a kingdom, priests unto His God and Father.'[8] As such a right of entrance into the divine Presence has been granted to us, a 'new and living way' opened, and by what means is implied in the writer's unusual use of a Greek word meaning 'newly-slain,' no doubt as a reference to the fact that our Lord Himself is the Way.

'Through the veil' which is His flesh, that is, His human nature. This may be called a veil in a double sense since it both hid His divinity and was the medium through which it was revealed. 'He that hath seen Me hath seen the Father.'[9] Also, it was in His human nature that He entered into His glory, and united to which, we have boldness to follow the way He has trodden before us.

And having a great priest over the house of God;

Great in person, in office, and in His supreme Headship over the whole household of God.[10] A great deal of modern

---

[1] Phil. iii. 20.   [2] Eph. i. 3.   [3] ibid., ii. 6.
[4] Heb. xii. 22.   [5] Cf. Eph. ii. 17—19.   [6] 2 S. Pet. i. 4.
[7] Rom. vi. 4.   [8] Rev. i. 6; cf. 1 S. Pet. ii. 5.
[9] S. John xiv. 9; i. 14.   [10] Cf. Eph. i. 22, 23.

Christian thought tends to emphasize the human, humble, tender side of our Lord's Person, and His relation to men, at the expense of His unique and awe-compelling Majesty. To keep a sense of balance and proportion in our thinking about the divine mysteries of the Faith is no doubt difficult, but it is necessary lest our whole view becomes onesided, and leads, as it has often done, to heresy. Church history shows a recurring swing of the pendulum between these two equally true conceptions of our Lord. The Early Church was driven to lay emphasis upon His Godhead, and in time this produced that Byzantine art, reflecting the thought of the age, in which He is represented as the Sovereign Lord and Judge of men, clothed in so unearthly and remote majesty as almost to forbid approach. The twelfth and thirteenth centuries produced a reaction which dwelt upon the sacred Humanity, and gave rise both to a tender devotion to Christ as Man, and to the exquisite and touching art of the Italian and Flemish schools. Both conceptions were saved from possible danger by the Church's possession of a sound theology of the Incarnation which acted as a balance operating upon the minds even of the more illiterate of the faithful to whom it was as little comprehended as it is to-day, though its conclusions were more firmly believed. The most human representation of Jesus, pictured in the homely and familiar surroundings of a Tuscan or Umbrian landscape, evoked a renewal of faith in, and devotion to, Him Who is the Word made flesh. But the divine condescension which has made it easy for us to obey His word, 'Come unto Me,' does not entitle us to forget Who it is to Whom we come, so that a tender and loving familiarity degenerates into pietistic impertinence.

Let us draw near with a true heart in fullness of faith, having our hearts sprinkled from an evil conscience, and our body washed with pure water; let us hold fast the confession of our hope that it waver not; for He is faithful that promised:

Our approach to the divine Presence must be dominated by faith, 'for he that cometh to God must believe that He is.'[1] Such 'fullness of faith' rests upon God's revelation of Himself in His Son, that is, upon facts openly manifested in the order of time and place, and attested by the witness of the Apostles.[2] Under the Law, as in all ancient religions, both priests and worshippers underwent a symbolical purification with water before worship,[3] but now it is the inner self, the heart and conscience, which is to be cleansed by the sprinkling of the Precious Blood which in Baptism and Penance is applied to the soul-body nature for the cleansing of the whole man.[4]

The confession of faith in Baptism, daily renewed in the recitation of the Creed, is also the confession of our hope, or, as the Nicene Creed puts it, our confident expectation of the fulfilment of the promises of God. Such hope, which admits of no doubt, and consequent wavering, is rooted in the fact that God is faithful to His promises, the earnest and pledge of which He has given to us, both in His Word and in the means of grace by which we already become partakers of divine realities.

And let us consider one another to provoke unto love and good works; not forsaking the assembling of ourselves together, as the custom of some is, but exhorting one another; and so much the more as ye see the Day approaching.

The order of charity is to be kept: love of God with its consequence of faith, hope, penitence, worship; use of the means of salvation; and then, love of our neighbour. 'Consider one another,' not as is so common, critically, enviously, jealously, and so provoking to evil, but in such ways as to arouse love, the doing of good, and the further-

---

[1] Heb. xi. 6.   [2] Cf. Acts ii. 32; 1 S. John i. 1.
[3] Exod. xxix. 1–4; Lev. xvi. 4.
[4] Titus iii. 5; cf. the prayer in the Blessing of the Font on Holy Saturday: 'Mercifully grant that the thirst of their faith may, by the mystery of Baptism, sanctify them in body and soul.'

H

ance of a sincere Christian fellowship which reaches its
highest expression in 'the assembly,' the gathering together
of the Christian people in the supreme act of unity and
worship, the Eucharist. This is as certainly what the
writer means as it has ever been, and is, the mind of the
Church.

The loss of the sense of the *obligation* of worship, which is
widespread even amongst professing Christians of to-day,
is one of the primary evils of our time. For it witnesses,
not only to a decay of faith, but also to a forgetfulness of
God, if not a contempt for Him, which results in a loss of
the sense of one's place before God, and in consequence,
of one's relation and obligations to one's fellow men. It
is not surprising that it is most common in the so-called
'democratic' states of to-day which, in greater or lesser
degree, are reflections of the totalitarian conception which,
far from uprooting, they are diligently preserving and
forcing upon their people. For when men forsake the
worship of God they can but fall into idolatry, and to-day
the state and the machine are their gods, both luring to
destruction.

'The Day' is that of the Second Advent, 'the day of the
Lord,' 'the day of Jesus Christ,' 'the great day' of judgement, and of the open fulfilment of the promises of God.
It is little wonder that the first Christians believed it to be
near at hand. They were words of our Lord,[1] which were
intended to refer both to this day and to that day of
crisis, the Roman attack upon, and destruction of,
Jerusalem consequent upon the Jewish revolt in A.D. 70,
rumours of the underground movement of which were
already spreading throughout the land. To forsake their
primary Christian duty in the face of such fears betokens
a lack of faith at a moment when nothing else would save
them from the terror which was near at hand. For every
such day, from that on which Jerusalem fell to such days
as we have lived through, is a portent and a warning of

[1] S. Matt. xxiv.

that final, inescapable Day which shall come as 'a thief in the night,' and for which coming faithfulness, watchfulness, and perseverance are the only preparation.

For if we sin wilfully after that we have received the knowledge of the truth, there remaineth no more a sacrifice for sins, but a certain fearful expectation of judgement, and a fierceness of fire which shall devour the adversaries. A man that hath set at nought Moses' law dieth without compassion on the word of two or three witnesses: of how much sorer punishment, think ye, shall he be judged worthy, who hath trodden under foot the Son of God, and hath counted the Blood of the Covenant, wherewith he was sanctified, an unholy thing, and hath done despite unto the Spirit of grace? For we know Him that said, Vengeance belongeth unto Me, I will recompense. And again, The Lord shall judge His people. It is a fearful thing to fall into the hands of the living God.

Like the passage in chapter vi, the sin here spoken of is that of apostasy from the Faith, the wilful rejection of the truth of which one has been convinced. It would, at first sight, appear to be one of the commonest sins of our time. But closer consideration of those who fall away from the Church into one of the many pseudo-Christian cults which are prevalent in our midst, will generally show that the main cause of their apostasy, for such it is, is the lack of any real knowledge of the Faith. Such ignorance, as common amongst the educated as the more illiterate, renders them easy victims to the propagators of cults so irrational, un-Christian, and foolish, that nothing else could explain the ease with which their pernicious teachings—based on no authority save that of some self-constituted interpreter of Holy Scripture who is ranked by his or her disciples as equal to our Lord, or even higher—gain adherence.

The implied impossibility of a return to the Faith of an apostate who has known and accepted it lies in the character of the sin itself, and does not constitute a denial, or limitation of the power of divine grace, nor of the power of the Church to absolve from all sins upon the repentance of the sinner. What the writer has in mind is a deliberate, considered act for which no repentance is manifested, and this is the reason why 'there remaineth no more sacrifice for sin,' since the sinner refuses to avail himself of the one prevailing Sacrifice of Christ. The reference in verse 28 is to Deuteronomy xvii. 2–7, which describes the mode of the death penalty to be inflicted on one who turns from the living God to worship idols. Now an idol is not merely a graven image of a false god, it is anything which a man puts first in his thought and life, and to which he gives himself and his service. Such idolatry of the mind is more common, and more dangerous, than that of some primitive image-worshipper.

And when we are tempted to regard the infliction of the death-penalty for the sin of apostasy, as far outweighing the offence, we shall do well to remember that it is still inflicted upon those guilty of murder of the body, and this for the protection of society, which was precisely the reason why it was the custom in days when religion was held to be the most important thing in the world, and the human soul of infinitely more value than the body. Thus the apostate was regarded, as we regard the criminal, as an enemy of society, and a danger who, if he did not repent, must suffer for the sake of the community.[1]

If, then, under the Law with which his readers were so familiar the apostate was liable to suffer physical death, how much greater penalty awaits him who, having been admitted into the New Covenant sealed by the Precious Blood, now treats it as that of a criminal, an unclean thing,

[1] The present writer must not be thought to be defending this practice as it was carried over into Christian times, both by Catholics and Protestants; he is only explaining the reason for its existence, and why it cannot, and ought not, to be summarily condemned by those who only view it from the standpoint of the present day, and often without any understanding of the real issues involved.

and rejects the light and grace of the Holy Spirit of God?
For we know that God is a righteous Judge, just no less than
merciful, One Who cannot be mocked with impunity,[1]
nor will stay His hand to prevent the unrepentant sinner
from reaping what he has sown. There is no justification
in Holy Scripture for the assumption that whatever life a
man has lived 'it will be all right in the end.' For the end
is the consequence of what has gone before, and formed
a man's character, made him what he is; and judgement
is no arbitrary sentence, but the divine acceptance of
what is. 'He that is unrighteous, let him be unrighteous
still: and he that is filthy let him be filthy still: and he
that is holy, let him be holy still.'[2] 'For our God is a
consuming fire' of such love as shall inflame the heart of
His lovers, and be as a devouring fire to those who have
despised it.

*But call to remembrance the former days, in which, after ye
were enlightened, ye endured a great conflict of sufferings; partly
being made a gazingstock both by reproaches and afflictions; and
partly, becoming partakers with them that were so used. For ye
both had compassion on them that were in bonds, and took
joyfully the spoiling of your possessions, knowing that ye yourselves have a better possession and an abiding one. Cast not
away, therefore, your boldness, which hath great recompense of
reward. For ye have need of patience, that, having done the will
of God, ye may receive the promise:*
    For yet a little while,
    He that cometh shall come, and shall not tarry.
    But My righteous one shall live by faith:
    And if he shrink back, My soul hath no pleasure in him.
    *But we are not of them that shrink back unto perdition; but of
them that have faith unto the saving of the soul.*

Swiftly the writer turns from warning to encouragement, and to his confidence in their steadfastness of which
they had given proof in the past. Illumined with the light

[1] Gal. vi. 7.   [2] Rev. xxii. 11.

of faith in Baptism, they had been exposed to the scorn
of their neighbours, and shared in the persecutions which
befell other converts to the new Faith. They had exhibited charity to those who were cast into prison, and
suffered the destroying and looting of their goods at the
hands of the mob. Glimpses of these events are given in
the Acts.[1]

It is very difficult for us, even when we read of similar
things in so many countries to-day, to realize what it
must mean, and what a test of faith it must be, to be in
daily, hourly, fear of both official and mob terrorism, to
be regarded as criminals, to have hanging over one the
possibility of imprisonment, torture, and death, such as
thousands of our fellow-Christians of almost every race
have had to face in the last few years, as indeed many
had done earlier. We are apt to congratulate ourselves
on our escape, but we would do well to ask ourselves
sometimes whether it may not be due to the fact that our
immediate world does not regard us as worth persecuting.
It does not hate us; is its contemptuous indifference any
comfort to our souls? The quotation with which this
passage ends is from Habakkuk ii. 1–4, in which the
prophet, viewing the victories of the Chaldeans over
Israel, is reassured by God, and bidden to await with
faith the final outcome of the struggle.

*Now faith is the assurance of things hoped for, the proving of
things not seen.*

Or we may translate, 'Faith is the substance of things
to be hoped for, the evidence of things that are unseen.'
The Greek word here translated 'substance' has been used
already in chapter i where it is said that the Son is 'the
very image of His substance,' where (as in the clause 'of
one substance with the Father' of the Nicene Creed) it
means of one nature, essence, life. In chapter iii the
same word is translated 'confidence,' 'if we hold fast the

[1] Acts viii. 1–3; ix. 28, 29; xii. 1, 2.

beginning of our confidence unto the end,' another common meaning of the Greek. Both meanings are contained in the present passage. Faith makes the hoped-for heavenly realities (which are existent and real independently of either our belief or our disbelief in them) existent and real *to us*, and so fills us with a strong confidence in them, and an assurance that we can rely upon, and live upon, our faith in them. For, as S. Thomas says, 'Faith draws divine things to us,' and causes them 'to abide in us.'[1] Thus our faith becomes evidence, proof of the existence and reality of things which lie beyond the reach of our senses, for we cannot see, hear, touch them in themselves, and even of our minds save as they are illumined, and their sight and apprehension extended, by faith.

Now all this splendid meaning, and quality of faith is obscured in our time, as it has been for some four hundred years, by Luther's error of making faith a feeling, an act of the emotions, instead of an act of the intellect, and by the common restriction of its meaning to a mere act of belief. The author of our Epistle, in common with the whole of the New Testament writers, makes it quite clear that by faith he means the acceptance by the mind of the word of God because it is the word of Him Who is supreme Truth. That word may be uttered directly, as to Moses, and by Christ to His disciples, or through divinely-chosen witnesses, as through the prophets of the Old Covenant, and through the Catholic Church which was the medium through which the first converts heard, and accepted, the Faith, and which is the one original source from which all our knowledge of Christianity is gained.

All the examples of faith which follow illustrate and develop the truth that it is an act of the intellect moved by the will; that it produces hope and confidence in the promises of God; and that it must be expressed in obedience, endurance, and perseverance.

[1] *On the Power of God*, Bk. II, Q. vi, art. 9.

By faith we understand that the worlds have been framed by the word of God, so that what is seen hath not been made out of things which do appear.

We must be careful to note that here faith is not contrasted with reason, but with experience. The distinction is important, for it is possible for human reason to demonstrate that the existence of the visible universe can only be rationally accounted for by that of a divine Creator. This fact is emphasized both by the author of the Book of Wisdom[1] and by S. Paul,[2] and the Christian philosophers, notably S. Thomas Aquinas, have shown the many ways in which the things of the visible creation lead to a rational conviction of, and belief in, the existence of God. But in the words before us the writer is contrasting our ordinary human experience that the visible things around us owe their existence to pre-existing visible things (for example, oaks from acorns, acorns from oaks) with the fact that the whole creation had its origin, not in some pre-existing matter, but solely in the divine *fiat* of God. Now of such an act of creation by which nothingness is succeeded by an existent, visible something (that is, the universe), of which the whole, both material and spiritual, is the work of God, we have no experience, nor can anything be told us by the physical scientist, who can only deal with what already exists. And whilst reason can help where experience fails us, only faith can enable us to accept the divine word, 'In the beginning God created the heavens and the earth.'[3]

By faith Abel offered unto God a more excellent sacrifice than Cain, through which he had witness borne to him that he was righteous. God bearing witness in respect of his gifts: and through it he being dead yet speaketh.

Abel's sacrifice was more excellent because it was actuated by a greater faith than that of Cain. We may

[1] Wisd. xiii. 1–9.   [2] Rom. i. 18–21.
[3] Gen. i. 1, etc.

compare the offering of the Eucharistic Sacrifice by two persons, one of whom is moved by a deep faith in God and in the virtue of the Sacrifice, the other who performs a duty with little realization of what he is doing. For whilst it is not the faith of the offerer which makes the sacrifice to be what it is, it is his faith which makes him a worthy offerer.

'Through it' may refer either to Abel's faith or to his sacrifice, probably to both since the latter was an outward manifestation of his faith. The account in Genesis iv does not show in what manner God made known His acceptance of Abel's sacrifice, but it does give us the reason for it in God's words to Cain, 'If thou doest well, shalt not thou be accepted, and if thou doest not well, sin lieth at the door.' Cain, instead of accepting this judgement upon his interior attitude, is filled with envy and jealousy which leads him to murder.

By faith Enoch was translated that he should not see death; and he was not found, because God translated him: for before his translation he hath had witness borne to him that he had been well-pleasing unto God: and without faith it is impossible to be well-pleasing unto Him: for he that cometh unto God must believe that He is, and that He is a rewarder of them that seek after Him.

The reference is to Genesis v. 22, 24. Enoch's faith was manifested in his life and actions, 'he walked with God,' in recollection of Him and obedience to His will. So to endeavour to please God in all things is a simpler and easier way to union with Him than a regard of, and seeking for, self-improvement.

'That he should not see death . . . and he was not.' We need not infer that he did not experience physical death. S. John records a similar use of the term 'see death' by our Lord, 'If a man keep My word, he shall never see death.'[1] Archbishop William Temple points out that the Greek word here translated 'never' is an

---

[1] S. John viii. 51.

unusual one, which means 'not unto eternity,' and that
the word 'see' implies close attention to, special notice
of, something. So if a man is occupied in keeping the
word of Christ death 'will matter no more to him than
the fall of a leaf from a tree under which he might be
reading a book. It happens to him, but he does not in
any full sense see or notice it.'[1]

We may assume, then, that Enoch, like our Lady,
experienced physical death and, like her, was translated
to heaven.

*By faith Noah, being warned of God concerning things not seen
as yet, moved with godly fear, prepared an ark to the saving of his
house; through which he condemned the world, and became heir
of the righteousness which is according to faith.*

Noah was the recipient of a special revelation concerning the judgement which was to befall the world of his
time, and what he must do to avoid being overtaken by
it. His faith moved him to filial fear in which, accepting
God's word, he built the ark, so condemning the un-
believing who 'aforetime were disobedient, when the
long-suffering of God waited in the days of Noah, while
the ark was a preparing.'[2] By his faith, witnessed to by
his obedience, 'he became heir of the righteousness' which
is the reward of faith.

*By faith Abraham, when he was called, obeyed to go out to a
place which he was to receive for an inheritance; and he went out,
not knowing whither he went. By faith he became a sojourner
in the land of promise, dwelling in tents, with Isaac and Jacob,
heirs with him of the same promise; for he looked for the city
which hath the foundations, whose builder and maker is God.*

The whole story of Abraham may be read in Genesis
xii–xxv. Its implications pervade the whole of the Old
and New Testaments. He occupies so large a place in

---

[1] *Readings in S. John's Gospel*, vol. i, p. 146.   [2] 1 S. Pet. iii. 20.

both Jewish and Christian thought that it is worth while to realize that the common conception of him as a primitive Bedouin chief is far from true. Any one who has walked through the ruined courtyards and palaces of Ur, or seen its golden treasures in the British Museum, will think of him as the citizen of a wealthy and highly-civilized city who, having accompanied his family to Haran, city and centre of the moon-worship of the Chaldeans, there heard and obeyed the call of God to abandon country and family, and at the age of seventy-five became 'a dweller in tents' and the father of a new people.

In this first reference to the faith which evoked his obedience to the call of God, a new characteristic of faith appears. Leaving the country of his birth he comes into the land of Canaan to which he has been promised the right of possession which, however, he does not yet enjoy, but in which he is a foreigner wandering about, and dwelling in tents. And this he does because his faith envisages more than that temporal possession which was to become his in his children. He has vision of a truer, abiding possession, of which the promised land was a figure and type; of a city eternal in the heavens, 'whose builder and maker is God,' and it is upon this that his faith ultimately rests.

By faith even Sarah herself received power to conceive seed when she was past age, since she counted Him faithful Who had promised: wherefore also there sprang from one, and him as good as dead, as many as the stars of heaven in multitude and as the sand, which is by the sea-shore, innumerable.

There are two accounts of this episode,[1] in the first of which Abraham's faith is said to have wavered, and in the second, that of his wife. This was hardly surprising under the circumstances, and our author assumes that Sarah's faith in the word of God was restored.

[1] Gen. xvii. 15–19; xviii. 1–15.

*These all died in faith, not having received the promises, but
having seen them and greeted them from afar, and having confessed that they were strangers and pilgrims on the earth. For
they that say such things make it manifest that they are seeking
after a country of their own. And if indeed they had been
mindful of that country from which they came out, they would
have had opportunity to return. But now they desire a better
country, that is, a heavenly: wherefore God is not ashamed to be
of them, to be called their God: for He hath prepared for them
a city.*

'These all' refers to the persons already mentioned,
from Abel to Abraham, who had died in the faith that
God would fulfil His promises made to Abraham and his
descendants. They had spoken of themselves as 'strangers
and pilgrims' who had no country of their own, for if
they had thought of Chaldea as their country, being
Abraham's birthplace, they could have returned there.
In the literal, historical sense the country they looked for
was the land of Canaan which later became theirs, but
symbolically this was a figure of man's true native country,
that Messianic kingdom of which the prophets speak so
plainly, and of which our Lord said, 'My kingdom is not
of this world.'[1]

'Wherefore God is not ashamed . . .' We may see a
double meaning in these words. First, that of which we
read in Exodus of God's word to Moses, 'I am the God of
thy father, the God of Abraham, Isaac, and Jacob';[2] and
second, the writer's own words in chapter ii. 11, 'He is
not ashamed to call them brethren,' since at the Incarnation He becomes one of their race.

*By faith Abraham, being tried, offered up Isaac: yea, he that
had gladly received the promises was offering up his only-begotten
son; even he of whom it was said, In Isaac shall thy seed be called:
accounting that God is able to raise up, even from the dead; from
whence he did also in a parable receive him back.*

[1] S. John xviii. 36.   [2] Exod. iii. 6, 15.

In Genesis xxii. 1 we read 'God did tempt Abraham,' whilst here we have 'Abraham being tried,' that is, tested. Now that 'tempted' is commonly understood to mean 'tempted to evil,' it must be remembered that, as S. James says, temptation in this sense must not be attributed to God 'for God cannot be tempted with evil, and He Himself tempteth no man.'[1] But He does test men, as the author of Ecclesiasticus writes of this particular case that 'when Abraham was proved he was found faithful.'[2] Abraham had already given proof of his faith and obedience, and this is now subjected to a final test, the severity of which lies in the fact that it appears to be contrary to the promise of God already made to him, that in him and his seed should all nations be blessed. Now the command to sacrifice Isaac, here named 'his only-begotten son,' in distinction from Ishmael, who was born out of wedlock, if obeyed, seems to nullify the hope he had been encouraged to cherish. Yet his faith in the word of God, strengthened perhaps by his remembrance of His words to Sarah, 'Is anything too hard for the Lord?'[3] triumphs, and as S. James says, he 'believed God and it was counted unto him for righteousness; and he was called the friend of God.'[4] We may note that S. James uses this test of Abraham as an example of the truth that faith must be exhibited by good works, 'faith wrought through his works, and by works was his faith made perfect.'

There is a Portuguese proverb which runs, 'God writes straight with crooked lines,' a truth which experience justifies. There are times when He leads a soul in a particular direction so that it may well be thought that He means one to reach a particular end. Then the direction is changed and another end indicated. The reason would seem to be that only by this crooked or, so to speak, roundabout way does God know that His design for the soul will be attained. It was so with our

---

[1] S. Jas. i. 13.   [2] Ecclus. xliv. 20.
[3] Gen. xviii. 14.   [4] S. Jas. ii. 20–24.

Lady, who was led to make a vow of virginity, then led into marriage, and finally to become the Virgin-Mother of God, which was the end He had in mind from the beginning.

So was it with Abraham who was led this way and that, but with one end always in view, that by his obedient faith in God he might become the father of many nations, and an example of what true faith really means.

The sense of the words 'in a parable' is not clear. 'Parable' may be used here as in ix. 9, as a synonym for 'type' or 'figure,' and if so would mean that Isaac's preservation from death was a type of the Resurrection. Or it may mean that whilst in intention Abraham gave up his son, yet in fact he received him back from death, and so Isaac is a type of Christ Who was really to be sacrificed and to rise from the dead. In this connection, the words of Genesis xxii. 8 are significant: 'God will provide Himself a lamb for a burnt-offering.'

By faith Isaac blessed Jacob and Esau, even concerning things to come. By faith Jacob, when he was a dying, blessed each of the sons of Joseph; and worshipped, leaning upon the top of his staff. By faith Joseph, when his end was nigh, made mention of the departure of the children of Israel; and gave commandment concerning his bones.

These three examples are taken together because they illustrate faith as resting upon the word of God, the fulfilment of which lay in the future. Thus the blessing conferred is also a prophecy and earnest of the certainty of good things to come. In the case of Joseph it concerned the future departure of the Israelites from Egypt. The accounts of these events are given in Genesis xxviii, xlix, and l.

By faith Moses, when he was born, was hid three months by his parents, because they saw that he was a goodly child; and they were not afraid of the king's commandment. By faith Moses, when he had grown up, refused to be called the son of Pharaoh's daughter; choosing rather to be evil entreated with the people of

God, than to enjoy the pleasures of sin for a season; accounting the reproach of Christ greater riches than the treasures of Egypt: for he looked unto the recompense of reward. By faith he forsook Egypt, not fearing the wrath of the king: for he endured, as seeing Him Who is invisible. By faith he kept the passover, and the sprinkling of the blood, that the destroyer of the firstborn should not touch them.

For the account of the events summarized here Exodus i–xiii inclusive should be read. The cardinal note of the whole passage is 'he endured, as seeing,' as if he actually saw, God, 'Who is invisible.' Because of this faith in which he looked 'not at the things which are seen, but at the things which are not seen,' at the eternal realities rather than the impermanent things of the temporal order,[1] he rejected rank, position, honours, and pleasure, in obedience to the call of God and embraced an arduous and demanding life which held no temporal reward in view. It is of the very essence of faith to act upon the conviction that God is the supreme Reality, the primary Fact with which we have to do. To such faith all things are possible; without it life and endeavour fall into disorder and the ruin which besets all temporal things. 'Except the Lord build the house, their labour is but lost that build it.'[2] Nothing could so expose the futility and foolishness of the call of certain politicians of our day 'to put our faith in the future' of temporal progress and prosperity. They have been answered already.[3]

By faith they passed through the Red sea as by dry land: which the Egyptians assaying to do were swallowed up. By faith the walls of Jericho fell down, after they had been compassed about for seven days. By faith Rahab the harlot perished not with them that were disobedient, having received the spies with peace.

We have here three examples of faith resting upon the word of those whom God had chosen to witness to Him, and to lead His people. Moses, Joshua, and the spies

[1] 2 Cor. iv. 18.   [2] Ps. cxxvii. 1.   [3] S. Matt. vii. 24–27.

who were sent to Jericho, and saved from discovery there by the harlot Rahab who confessed, 'The Lord your God, He is God in heaven above, and in earth beneath.'[1] She was, in consequence of her sheltering the spies, spared in the destruction which befell the city,[2] and by becoming the wife of one Salmon,[3] and so an ancestress of David, finds her place in our Lord's genealogy.

And what shall I more say? for the time will fail me if I tell of Gideon, Barak, Samson, Jephthah; of David and Samuel and the prophets: who through faith subdued kingdoms, wrought righteousness, obtained promises, stopped the mouths of lions, quenched the power of fire, escaped the edge of the sword, from weakness were made strong, waxed mighty in war, turned to flight armies of aliens.

There was no need for the writer to be more precise, and to go into details of which his readers were so familiar. 'Subdued kingdoms' would remind them of Joshua, the Judges, and David. 'Wrought righteousness' of Samuel;[4] 'obtained promises' probably refers to the fulfilment of God's promises to Abraham; 'stopped the mouths of lions' to Daniel;[5] 'quenched the power of fire' to the three children cast into the furnace.[6] 'Escaped the edge of the sword,' etc., may refer to David, or be a general allusion to more than one person.

Women received their dead by a resurrection: and others were tortured, not accepting deliverance; that they might obtain a better resurrection; and others had trial of mockings and scourgings, yea, moreover, of bonds and imprisonments: they were stoned, they were sawn asunder, they were tempted, they were slain with the sword: they went about in sheepskins, in goatskins; being destitute, afflicted, evil entreated (of whom the world was not worthy), wandering in deserts, mountains, and caves, and the holes of the earth.

[1] Joshua ii.   [2] ibid., vi.   [3] S. Matt. i. 5.
[4] Cf. 1 Kings xii. 4.   [5] Dan. vi. 22.   [6] ibid., iii. 27.

The writer may have had particular examples of faithfulness in his mind, as, for example, the widow of Zarephath;[1] Eleazar;[2] the seven brothers and their mother;[3] Jeremiah;[4] Zechariah;[5] Isaiah, who tradition said was sawn asunder; prophets.[6]

And these all, having had witness borne to them through their faith, received not the promise, God having provided some better thing concerning us, that apart from us they should not be made perfect.

The promises of the Old Testament are fulfilled in the New Covenant inaugurated by Jesus Christ, the promised Messiah, the hope of Israel, to Whom all the Old Testament points, and of Whose coming, and the establishment of Whose kingdom, the Church, the prophets bore witness. The Old Covenant spoke of and typified the true end and perfection of man, but could not accomplish it. Only in communion with the mystical Body of Christ on earth could Jews be perfected with those who by Baptism are united to 'the Author and Perfecter' of faith.

The word 'perfect,' which is used in more than one sense in this Epistle, here refers to the final perfecting of our body-soul nature which will be accomplished at the general resurrection.

Therefore let us also, seeing we are compassed about with so great a cloud of witnesses, lay aside every weight, and the sin which doth so easily beset us, and let us run with patience the race that is set before us.

These words are often taken to have been suggested by the thought of a Greek or Roman arena, or 'sports stadium,' in which the competitors in a race are encouraged by the cheers of the spectators seated above and

[1] 1 Kings xvii.
[2] 2 Macc. vi. 18 ff.
[3] ibid., vii.
[4] Jer. xxxviii. 6.
[5] 2 Chron. xxiv. 20, 21.
[6] 1 Kings xviii. 4; xvii. 2–5; xix. 4.

I

around the ground in which the sports take place. But
it is at least doubtful whether this was in the writer's
mind, and it is not borne out by what he says. For such
sports were regarded with abhorrence by the Jews;
the introduction of Greek customs under Antiochus
Epiphanes (168 B.C.), including a gymnasium,[1] was the
main cause of the Maccabean revolt. It seems unlikely
that a Jewish Christian writing to Jewish converts would
use such an illustration particularly when he had just
been reminding them of those who had suffered in fighting
against such innovations which carried with them some
participation in pagan ceremonies. Nor, indeed, does he
do so. He speaks of a 'cloud of witnesses' not in the sense
of 'spectators' looking on at what is passing before them,
but as bearing witness by their faith and obedience and
sufferings to God and His word. This primary idea does
not exclude the more common interpretation altogether, for
he goes on to speak of the Christian as an athlete running
a race.[2] But the encouragement which is offered by the
heroes of the past derives, not from what they may now
be doing, but from the faith to which they have witnessed.
No doubt Christians are aided by the prayers of the saints,
but that is not what the writer says, or means, here. The
Greek word for 'witness' is martyr, which bears the sense
of an open, public witness to some truth or cause, such as
Christians have given from the earliest days unto our own
time. And it is worth noting that the majority of them
were, and are, just ordinary men and women who prac-
tised their religion in such a way as to afford no particular
notice, but who, when faced with torture and death, did
so bravely and quietly in witness to their faith.

It is well to remember also that for the first three
hundred years large numbers of them thus suffered because, in defiance of the State, they persisted in obeying
their Lord's command, 'Do this in remembrance of Me,'

[1] 1 Macc. i. 14.
[2] Cf. similar comparisons in 1 Cor. ix. 24; Phil. iii. 14; 1 Tim. vi. 12.

a command which to-day so many ignore, or treat as a matter of their own choice and convenience.

'Laying aside every weight,' everything which would hinder one from running 'in the way of' God's commandments,[1] things which however innocent in themselves yet may easily become hindrances to our Christian progress. 'And the sin . . .' the clinging, encumbering habit of sin which is always tripping us up. 'Let us run with' patient endurance, one of the virtues most necessary, for this 'race is not to the swift, nor the battle to the strong,'[2] but to him that perseveres unto the end.[3] 'Everywhere thou must of necessity hold fast patience, if thou desirest inward peace, and wouldest merit an eternal crown.'[4] The Greek word here translated 'race' has the sense of a contest to be met, endured, and so won.

Looking unto Jesus the author and perfecter of our faith, Who for the joy that was set before Him endured the Cross, despising shame, and hath sat down at the right hand of the throne of God.

There is nothing in this passage, whether we read 'our faith' or simply 'faith,' which implies that our Lord possessed and exercised faith in the strict sense of the word. For even in His life on earth He enjoyed the fullness of the Beatific Vision of God.[5] His trust and confidence in the Father were consequence of His knowledge, not of faith such as is ours. He is the author, or leader, and perfecter of the faith which enables us to accept His word as that of very God Himself. 'Ye believe in God, believe also in Me.'[6]

For consider Him that hath endured such gainsaying of sinners against themselves [or Himself], *that ye wax not weary, fainting in your souls.*

---

[1] Ps. cxix. 32.   [2] Eccles. ix. 11.
[3] S. Matt. xxiv. 13.   [4] *Imitation*, I. xii. 4.
[5] Cf. S. John i. 18; iii. 13; vii. 29; x. 15; Col. ii. 3, 9.
[6] S. John xiv. 1.

'Look unto . . . consider' Jesus. The Greek word means not merely to look at, but to look into, to gaze repeatedly and intently so as to grasp the significance of what one is looking at. So are we to consider, think about, meditate upon, Jesus. Such looking at, and considering, of Jesus as He is shown to us in Holy Scripture is necessary if we are, as He bids us, to learn of and follow Him. S. Teresa says that much of our stumbling and falling is due to our 'not fixing our gaze on Him Who is the Way.' To contemplate Him, to listen to His words, watch His acts, meditate upon the mysteries of His divine-human life, all this is to place ourselves in the Light and Life and Love which He is, so that the rays of that Light, the power of that Life, the fire of that Love may illumine our minds, strengthen our wills, and inflame our hearts.

Here, it is the sufferings of Jesus which we are asked to consider. It would seem that 'against Himself' would be the most natural reading, but 'against themselves' is found in many manuscripts and does convey a truth not to be forgotten. For the consequences of sin are more harmful to the sinner than to him who is sinned against. In crucifying our Lord the Jews lost the one hope of salvation; the curse they invoked upon themselves[1] speedily fell upon, and still falls upon, them.

For you have not yet resisted unto blood, striving against sin;

Not, probably, sin in general, but the particular sin of apostasy against which he is mainly concerned to warn them. This they had so far resisted but not up to the possible point of torture and death, as our Lord had done.

And ye have forgotten the exhortation which reasoneth with you as sons,
> *My son, regard not lightly the chastening of the Lord,*
> *Nor faint when thou art reproved of Him:*
> *For whom the Lord loveth He chasteneth,*

[1] S. Matt. xxvii. 25.

And scourgeth every son whom He receiveth.
It is for chastening that you endure; God dealeth with you as sons;
for what son is there whom his father chasteneth not? But if ye
are without chastening, whereof all hath been made partakers, then
are ye bastards, and not sons.

The quotation is from Proverbs iii. 11, 12. Their
sufferings under persecution are not to be regarded as a
punishment, but as training, discipline, the perfecting
of their faith, hope, and charity. It is a token of God's
love for them, and of His design for them. So do fathers
correct and train their sons, desiring only their good.

Yet even professing Christians may be found saying, 'I
don't know why God allows me to suffer; I'm sure I've
done nothing to deserve it.' True or not as the latter may
be, the attitude of mind is all wrong, and shows little
appreciation of what God is, and an ignorance of the
teaching of Holy Scripture upon the subject of suffering
and its end. Too many people expect that the object of
the Christian religion is to make life easier, and more
comfortable, a belief for which there is not the slightest
warrant in the Bible, especially in the New Testament.
'If thou come to serve the Lord, prepare thy soul for
temptation [i.e. trials]. Set thy heart aright, and constantly endure.'[1] 'Blessed are they which are persecuted
for righteousness sake.'[2] 'Think not that I am come to
send peace upon the earth: I came not to send peace but
a sword.'[3] 'In the world ye shall have tribulation.'[4]

Furthermore, we had fathers of our flesh to chasten us, and we
gave them reverence; shall we not much rather be in subjection to
the Father of spirits, and live? For they verily for a few days
chastened us as seemed good to them; but He for our profit, that
we may be partakers of His holiness.

The purpose of God's allowing suffering, whatever the
cause and nature of it may be, is clearly stated. It is, that

[1] Ecclus. ii. 1, 2, etc.   [2] S. Matt. v. 10.   [3] ibid., x. 34.
[4] S. John xvi. 33; cf. xv. 20; and many similar words.

we 'may live,' 'for our profit,' 'that we may be partakers of His holiness.' It is never for the crushing or inhibiting of life, but to bring us to the fullness of life. This applies to every kind of self-discipline and mortification as to that which comes from outside ourselves. It is for our spiritual life what physical training is for our body, to make us fit, to develop the whole of our faculties, and bring the warring parts of our nature into unity, and direction to one end. So may we become sharers in the wholeness of God, 'filled with all the fullness of God,'[1] 'in Him' in Whom we 'are made full.'[2] This is the perfection which the Law could not effect, but did foreshadow, and now is made possible by Him Who came to fulfil the Law.[3]

All chastening seemeth for the present to be not joyous, but grievous; yet afterward it yieldeth peaceable fruit unto them that have been exercised thereby, even the fruit of righteousness. Wherefore lift up the hands that hang down, and the palsied knees; and make straight paths for your feet, that that which is lame be not turned out of the way, but rather be healed.

There is no need to pretend that we *like* chastisement; our Lord shrank from it, 'If it be possible, let this cup pass from Me.' It is not a question of liking but of willing. 'Nevertheless, not My will, but Thine, be done.'[4]

'Lift up the hands . . .' probably a remembrance of Isaiah xxxv. 3. Put aside your fears and indecision, and with courage 'make straight paths with your feet,' that those who are halting in the way may be strengthened by your example.

Follow after peace with all men, and the sanctification without which no man shall see the Lord: looking carefully lest there be any man that falleth short of the grace of God:

The first clause concerns the Christian's duty towards his fellows; the second, that toward himself. Both are to

[1] Eph. iii. 19.   [2] Col. ii. 10.
[3] S. Matt. v. 17; cf. Rom. x. 4.   [4] S. Luke xxii. 42.

be actively pursued, not one at the expense of the other. 'Blessed are the peacemakers'[1] says our Lord, and this, like the other Beatitudes, would be a better subject for self-examination than many which are often used.

> Make me an instrument of Thy peace;
> Where there is hatred, let me sow love;
> Where there is injury, pardon;
> Where there is discord, union;
> Where there is doubt, faith;
> Where there is despair, hope;
> Where there is darkness, light:
> Where there is sadness, joy.[2]

We have spoken of holiness as 'wholeness,' the gathering together and ordering of our whole being. This can only come as the culmination of a positive seeking after conformity to Jesus, Who is the Image in which we were created, and by Whom we are to be renewed 'in the spirit of our minds.'[3] 'Let us cleanse ourselves from all defilement of flesh and spirit, perfecting holiness in the fear of the Lord.'[4]

'Looking carefully . . .' The word implies that one is in a position in which such a regarding of others is a duty. If it is not, we must beware of the common temptation of paying more attention to the lives and doings of others than to ourselves.[5] Too many people want to reform their neighbours, forgetting that the only reformers who have accomplished any good began with themselves.

S. Paul speaks of all men as falling 'short of the glory of God';[6] here it is a case of not corresponding with that grace which is the seed and earnest of glory.

Lest any root of bitterness springing up trouble you, and thereby the many be defiled;

[1] S. Matt. v. 9.
[2] Attributed to S. Francis of Assisi.
[3] Eph. iv. 24; Col. iii. 10.
[4] 2 Cor. vii. 1.
[5] S. Matt. vii. 1–5.
[6] Rom. iii. 23.

Some cause of bitter, angry, jealous feelings within the soul, so dwelt upon and cherished that it breaks out in words and acts, and causes scandal, and the comment, once uttered in wonder, but now so often in scorn, 'See how these Christians love one another.'

Lest there be any fornicator, or profane person, as Esau, who for one mess of meat sold his own birthright. For ye know that even afterward when he desired to inherit the blessing, he was rejected (for he found no place of repentance), though he sought it diligently with tears.

All through Holy Scripture the word 'fornication' is used both of the physical sin and of the spiritual sin of idolatry. Here it may mean the former, but the context would seem to indicate the latter, and in particular the act of one who had, or was in danger of, selling his Christian birthright by relapsing into Judaism. Esau had shown himself to be 'a profane person' in that he had no regard to the promise attached to him as the firstborn son of Isaac. That he 'found no place of repentance' applies only to the act of renunciation of his birthright. That act was irrevocable, he could not regain the birthright which he had thrown away. However genuine a repentance may be, it cannot alter the factual result of a sin, although it does alter one's attitude toward it.

For ye are not come unto a mount that might be touched, and that burnt with fire, and unto blackness, and darkness, and tempest, and the sound of a trumpet, and the voice of words; which voice they that heard intreated that no word more should be spoken unto them; for they could not endure that which was enjoined, If even a beast touch the mountain, it shall be stoned; and so fearful was the appearance, that Moses said, I exceedingly fear and quake.

The reference is to the account of the proclamation of the Law in Exodus xix. 10–25; xx. 18–21, and Deutero-

nomy iv. 11, 36; v. 4, 5, 22–26. The words attributed to
Moses do not occur in these accounts, and are probably
derived from some unrecorded tradition.

*But ye are come unto Mount Zion, and unto the city of the living
God, the heavenly Jerusalem, and to innumerable hosts of angels,
to the general assembly and church of the firstborn who are
enrolled in heaven, and to God the Judge of all, and to the spirits
of just men made perfect, and to Jesus the Mediator of a New
Covenant, and to the blood of sprinkling which speaketh better
things than that of Abel.*

The whole passage from verse 18 to verse 24 is designed
to emphasize the contrast between the Old and the New
Covenant, between the partial and preparatory revelation
made in physical and material circumstances and setting,
inspiring awe and fear, and that full revelation which, by
its very character, not only drew men to Him Who proclaimed it, but also did for them what the former one was
incapable of doing. The Israelites had shrunk back from
Sinai; the Holy Place of the Temple on Mount Zion, on
which the earthly Jerusalem sat in its pride, was closed to
them, but (and what more significant 'but' has ever been
uttered?) Christians have come already to the true and
eternal Zion,[1] and to 'myriads of angels in festal assembly,'
and to the whole Church of the firstborn children of God
in heaven and earth,[2] whose names are written in heaven,[3]
and to the God of all as Judge, and to the spirits of such
just men as have been mentioned in chapter xi who 'apart
from us could not be made perfect,' but now share in that
perfection which Christ has made possible,[4] and to Jesus
the true Mediator of the New Covenant 'counted worthy
of more glory than Moses,' mediator of the Old Covenant,
and to the sprinkling of the Precious Blood which, unlike
that of Abel, cries not for vengeance but for mercy. So is

[1] Cf. Gal. iv. 26; Rev. iii. 12; xxi. 2.
[2] Cf. S. Jas. i. 18, 'that we should be a kind of beginning of His creatures.'
[3] Cf. Mal. iii. 16; Rev. xx. 12–15.   [4] Cf. 1 S. Pet. iii. 19.

the substance, the present, accessible reality of truth and grace, contrasted with the shadow, the forecast and promise of 'good things to come.'

See that ye refuse not Him that speaketh. For if they escaped not, when they refused Him that warned them on earth, how much more shall not we escape, who turn away from Him that warneth from heaven: Whose voice then shook the earth: but now He hath promised, saying, Yet once more will I make to tremble not the earth only, but also the heaven. And this word, Yet once more, signifieth the removing of those things which are shaken, as of things which have been made, that those things which are not shaken may remain. Wherefore, receiving a kingdom which cannot be shaken, let us have grace, whereby we may offer service well-pleasing to God, with reverence and awe: for our God is a consuming fire.

The previous warnings against unbelief are repeated, and underlined by a reference to the fate of the Israelites who were not allowed to enter the promised land, but perished in the wilderness, which was the testing ground of their faith.[1]

The first 'Him' in the second sentence refers to God, not to Moses, for it was God Whom the people begged that they might not hear.[2] The contrast between 'on earth' and 'from heaven' is drawn from the fact that on Sinai God spake through a man, Moses, but now speaks through His Son Whose origin is from heaven.[3] There is a further contrast between the transitory character of the Old Covenant and the permanent character of the new one revealed by Christ. This second shaking, foretold by the prophet Haggai,[4] effected the removal of the things of the Covenant made on Sinai, an outward sign of which was the rending of the veil of the Temple, and the earthquake which marked the sealing of the New Testament with the death of Christ.[5]

'Let us have grace' may mean 'Let us give thanks,'

[1] Deut. viii. 2, 3; i. 19-40.   [2] Exod. xx. 19.
[3] Heb. i. 1, 2.   [4] Hag. ii. 6, 7.   [5] S. Matt. xxvii. 50-53.

but more likely, the grace of the Christian Faith, and of that kingdom 'which cannot be shaken.' For it is by grace, whether we think of it in the sense of the gracious-ness of God made known to us in His Son, or in the now more common sense of that sanctifying grace by which we are made 'partakers of the divine nature,'[1] that we become such as may 'offer service well-pleasing to God,' inspired to inward 'reverence and awe' as we approach 'our God' Who is none other than He Who of old revealed Himself as 'a consuming fire,' and Who now, as then, will not suffer Himself to be mocked, but must be worshipped in spirit and in truth.[2]

Let love of the brethren continue. Forget not to show love to strangers: for thereby some have entertained angels unawares. Remember them that are in bonds, as bound with them; them that are evil-entreated as being yourselves in the body.

The injunction to show love to strangers, coupled with 'love of the brethren,' shows of how practical a character it is to be,[3] and how little it has to do with 'liking.' Who knows whether in responding to a beggar's cry for help we may not, like Abraham and Lot,[4] be entertaining angels unawares, or, perchance, the Lord Himself?[5]

Let marriage be had in honour among all, and let the bed be undefiled: for fornicators and adulterers God will judge.

'Among all,' better 'in every respect.' The admonition is concerned with any unchastity in married couples.

Be ye free from the love of money, content with such things as ye have: for Himself hath said, I will in no wise fail thee, neither will I in any wise forsake thee. So that with good courage we say,
 The Lord is my helper; I will not fear:
 What shall man do unto me?

As in 1 Timothy vi. 10, it is the love of money, as displayed in avarice and covetousness, 'which some reach-

---

[1] 2 S. Pet. i. 4.　　[2] S. John iv. 23.　　[3] Cf. S. Jas. ii. 14–16.
[4] Gen. xviii. 3; xix. 2.　　　　[5] S. Matt. xxv. 31–46.

ing after have been led astray from the Faith,' which they
are warned against. The Christian will do well to make
his own the prayer of Agur, 'Give me neither poverty
nor riches; feed me with food convenient for me: lest I
be full and deny Thee, and say, Who is the Lord? or lest
I be poor, and steal, and take the name of my God in
vain.'[1] For 'godliness with contentment is great gain.'[2]

*Remember them that had the rule over you, which spake unto you
the word of God; and considering the issue of their life, imitate their
faith. Jesus Christ is the same yesterday, and to-day, and for ever.*

'Those who had rule . : .' are obviously the Apostles
from whom they had received the Faith, and who now
had either been martyred, as had S. Stephen and
S. James, or had gone to proclaim the Gospel in other
parts of the world. Their lives had been rooted in faith,
and it is such faith which his readers are to imitate since
He in Whom it was founded is, and will be, ever the same.
Thus the affirmation looks, not only to what has been
said, but also to what follows.

*Be not carried away by divers and strange teachings: for it is
good that the heart be stablished by grace; not by meats, wherein
they that occupied themselves were not profited. We have an
altar, whereof they have no right to eat which serve the tabernacle.*

The reference is both to those Judaizing elements who
wished to retain certain Jewish customs in Christianity,
and to those who were still Jews and were tempting
Christians to return to the ancient Faith by pointing to
the 'meats,' that is, the sacrificial rites offered in the
Temple. We can imagine them taunting Jewish Christians with comparisons between the worship of the Temple
and their own seemingly meagre and hole-and-corner
services held in private houses, and always in danger of
being broken up by the police or the mob. 'Do not be led
astray,' says the writer; 'the grace of your Christian Faith

[1] Prov. xxx. 8, 9.   [2] 1 Tim. vi. 6.

is infinitely greater than these Jewish rites which are no longer of value. Be firm in that Faith and the grace it affords you, for "We have an altar . . ." and a sacrificial meal which is beyond all price.'

Whether the term 'altar' is here used of Christ Himself, or of the Cross, or of the Christian altar on which the Eucharist is offered and becomes the Food of our souls, makes no difference to the obvious meaning which the writer intends to convey. For Christ is the Altar as He is the Priest and Victim, Who having made oblation of Himself in the Upper Room, consummates His Sacrifice upon the altar of the Cross, and is daily offered in and by His Mystical Body upon the altars of our churches, so becoming both our Sacrifice and our Food, 'the living bread which cometh down from heaven,' so that as He lives because of the Father, so he that eateth Me, he also shall live because of Me.'[1]

For the bodies of those beasts whose blood is brought into the holy place by the high priest as an offering for sin, are burned without the camp. Wherefore Jesus also, that He might sanctify the people through His own Blood, suffered without the gate. Let us therefore go forth unto Him without the camp, bearing His reproach. For we have not here an abiding city, but we seek after the city which is to come.

The time has come for Christians to make a clean, and decisive, break with Judaism. In the early days the Apostles had used the Temple for prayer and teaching, and had wrought many miracles there,[2] and it is likely that Christians had followed their example. But this was no longer possible, in fact it had become a danger from which flight was necessary. Let them remember how on the Day of Atonement the flesh of the beasts, whose blood the high priest sprinkled in the Holy of holies, was not eaten, as in other sacrifices, but burnt outside the camp in the wilderness, and outside the city in later times.

[1] S. John vi. 51, 57.   [2] Acts ii. 46; iii. 1; v. 12 ff.

This was a symbolic act expressive of the removal of sin
from the people, and is here interpreted of Christ, 'the
Lamb of God which taketh away the sin of the world,'
Who was crucified outside the city,[1] and Who, unlike the
Jewish sin-offering, was to be eaten by the faithful, as
being not only a sacrifice for sin, but also the chief means
of their sanctification.

'Let us go forth . . .,' no longer regarding Jerusalem
as the city of God, and of Israel's hope, to seek that city
'whose builder and maker is God.'   And indeed but a
short time was to elapse before not a trace of city or temple
remained, whilst the *Civitas Dei*, the new People of God,
after bearing the reproach of Christ for three centuries,
revealed itself as built upon a rock more enduring than
that of Zion of old.

*Through Him, then, let us offer up a sacrifice of praise con-
tinually, that is, the fruit of lips which make confession to His
Name.   But to do good and to communicate forget not: for
with such sacrifices God is well pleased.*

From the supreme act of Christian praise and thanks-
giving the writer turns to that continuous praise which the
whole life ought to express, and which rises to the lips in
our private devotions.   The phrase 'fruit of the lips' is
to be found in the Greek version of Hosea xiv. 2, and is
suggested by the fact that the Jewish sacrifice of thanks-
giving consisted of the fruits of the earth.[2] 'To communicate,' to do good to others, another reminder of the duty
of practical charity.

*Obey them that have the rule over you, and submit to them: for they
watch over your souls, as they that shall give account; that they may
do this with joy, and not with grief: for this were unprofitable for you.*

This admonition is based on the fact that their priests
possessed, and were appointed by, an apostolic authority
derived from our Lord Himself.[3]

[1] S. John xix. 20.   [2] Deut. xxvi.
[3] Cf. S. Luke x. 16; 2 Tim. i. 6; ii. 2; Titus i. 5; ii. 15.

Pray for us: for we are persuaded that we have a good conscience, desiring to live honestly in all things. And I exhort you the more exceedingly to do this, that I may be restored to you the sooner.

This, with verses 22, 23, is the only directly personal note in the Epistle, and indicates, as does the whole tone of the Epistle, that he held some position of authority which gave him the right to so address them.

Now the God of peace, Who brought again from the dead the great shepherd of the sheep with the blood of the eternal covenant, even our Lord Jesus, make you perfect in every good thing to do His will, working in us that which is well-pleasing in His sight, through Jesus Christ, to Whom be the glory for ever and ever. Amen.

The whole sentence is very Pauline in character. The invocation to 'the God of peace' is found in other Epistles.[1] The prayer for their perfection is reminiscent of Colossians i. 28; iv. 12; 1 Thessalonians iii. 10; and the latter part of the sentence finds a parallel in Philippians ii. 13.

The argument, the warnings, the exhortations reach their conclusion, the record of the act of God on our behalf is summed up. It is He Who 'is our peace,'[2] Who promised peace by His prophets of old time,[3] and both proclaimed and established it in His Son, 'the Prince of Peace.'[4] But let it not be imagined that this 'peace of God which passeth all understanding'[5] is one such as the world dreams of, and even now is thinking to bring about. Our Lord is explicit in declaring, 'I came not to bring peace, but a sword,'[6] and His discourse to His Apostles on the Mount of Olives[7] paints a very different picture from that so popular with our statesmen and politicians, as do His words in the Upper Room, 'Peace I leave with you; My peace I give unto you: not as the world giveth, give I unto you.'[8] His peace was announced to 'men of

---

[1] Rom. xv. 33; xvi. 20; 2 Cor. xiii. 11; 1 Thess. v. 23.   [2] Eph. ii. 14.
[3] Num. xxv. 12; Ps. xxix. 11; lxxxv. 8; Isa. liv. 13; Ezek. xxxiv. 25, etc.
[4] Isa. ix. 6.   [5] Phil. iv. 7.   [6] S. Matt. x. 34.
[7] S. Mark xiii.   [8] S. John xiv. 27.

goodwill,'[1] not to those who when He speaks to them of peace 'make them ready to battle.'[2] It is the peace which must first find place in the minds and hearts of men, establishing therein 'the tranquillity of order' before it can reign in the world.

> May peace from Thine own kingdom come to us,
> for with all reach of soul that in us lies
> we cannot win it, if it come not thus.[3]

It is that peace won by 'the blood of the eternal covenant,' with the fact of which the Epistle is all-concerned, whose one and final end is to 'perfect forever them that are sanctified.' To that perfection there is but one way, the doing of the divine will, in which alone is our peace. 'Not every one that saith unto Me, Lord, Lord, shall enter into the kingdom of heaven; but he that doeth the will of My Father Who is in heaven.'[4]

But I exhort you, brethren, bear with the word of exhortation; for I have written to you in few words. Know ye that our brother Timothy hath been set at liberty; with whom, if he come shortly, I will see you.

Salute all them that have the rule over you, and all the saints. They of Italy salute you. Grace be with you all. Amen.

A postscript commending this brief word of exhortation and consolation to his readers. We do not know the circumstances or place of Timothy's imprisonment, but the special mention of him, and of his approaching visit, suggests that he, like the writer, was known to the readers.

So with the usual remembrance to others our anonymous author disappears from sight, leaving nothing but this Epistle—but how much that is!—to those who in all ages share his faith and have cause to be grateful to him for his teaching, and for the encouragement to that steadfastness and perseverance which is no less necessary to us than to those who first read and pondered his words.

---

[1] S. Luke ii. 14.   [2] Ps. cxx. 6.
[3] Dante, *Purg.* xi. 7.   [4] S. Matt. vii. 21.

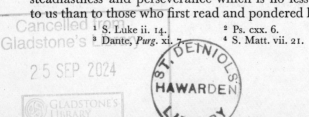